MAKING PATCHWORK
FOR PLEASURE & PROFIT

PAULINE BURBIDGE

MAKING PATCHWORK

FOR PLEASURE & PROFIT

JOHN GIFFORD

125 Charing Cross Road, London, WC2.

ISBN 0-7071-0633-8

© Pauline Burbidge 1981

First published 1981 by
John Gifford Ltd.,
125 Charing Cross Road,
London WC2 0EB

Photoset by Photobooks (Bristol) Ltd.
Printed and bound in Great Britain by
The Pitman Press, Bath

To Ross

ACKNOWLEDGEMENTS

I would like to thank the following people, for allowing me to re-claim their quilts to photograph and use in this book:

Angelo Cinque—Egyptian Quilt I (Scarab).
Mr and Mrs Aish—'Flying Ducks' quilt.
Mrs Kniestedt—Kaleidoscope Variation and the Fruit Basket wallhanging.
Jenny and Alec Hutchison—Large Fruit Basket Quilt.
Pat Jonas—Peacock Quilt.
Gail Jenkins—Small Egyptian Quilt.

I would like to give a special thankyou to Jenny and Alec Hutchison and Joen Lask. Also to Beth and Jeffrey Gutcheon, Dierdre Amsden, Michele Walker, Ron Simpson, Paul Taylor, Jim Nelson and The Crafts Council, and many other people who have helped and supported me, I am most grateful.

CONTENTS

COLOUR PLATES

INTRODUCTION

I began making patchwork quilts after having studied fashion
at art school. I designed clothes for some time after leaving
college but was disillusioned with its limitations. As usual in
the creative sense, it was always a battle between good design
and what was commercially viable. Also I was becoming very
tired of always designing something to fit the human form
and wanted to use fabric and colour in a more basic way.
Therefore, it seemed logical to work upon a relatively flat
surface. From this, I drew the conclusion that I should make
patchwork quilts. It seemed a good pure way of still using the
medium of fabric and colour.
I set about designing and making my first patchwork quilt
basing it on a traditional American block form. To guide me,
I had stumbled upon a book on patchwork in a junk shop
and was ever grateful to the mine of information that was
within that book. It was a book called 'Patchwork Quilts and
the Women who made them' by Ruth Finley. I was just really
lucky to have found it, especially at this particular moment in
my career. Anyway from the moment of making my first
patchwork quilt I could tell there was no going back. I was
completely hooked! Although my first quilt was very ordinary
and by no means a work of art, it set me thinking about the
endless possibilities that could be achieved.

I was first influenced very much by the American quilting
tradition, and my earlier work was often based on one or two
traditional block designs, of which there are endless variations
and just hundreds of different ways of putting them together.
When a quilt is made, it is always individual even if two
people make the same design. They will always choose
different fabric and the stitches will vary.

'How much piecin' a quilt is like livin' a life! You can give the
same kind of pieces to two persons, and one will make a
"nine-patch" and one'll make a "wild goose chase", and there
will be two quilts made out of the same kind of pieces, and
jest as different as they can be. And that is jest the way with

livin'. The Lord sends us pieces, but we can cut them out and put 'em together pretty much to suit ourselves, and there's a heap more in the cuttin' and the sewin' than there is in the caliker.' Eliza Calvert Hall in 'Aunt Jane of Kentucky'. Quoted from, 'The Romance of the patchwork quilt in America', by Carrie A. Hall and Rose G. Kretsinger.

So many of the old quilts were made very thriftily out of whatever fabric could be salvaged out of worn-out clothes. So the wardrobe of one household was always different from the next. We really have no excuse for not producing really stunning quilts today, with the availability and choice of fabric that we have at our fingertips now!

Gaining further interest in the subject, I bought more books and was delighted with the work that I saw. I found the quilts made by the Amish people beautiful and with such an unusual sense of design and colour that they inspired me tremendously. The Amish are a group of people living in and around the areas of Pennsylvania, Ohio, Indiana, Illinois, Missouri and Iowa, who have a long history of quiltmaking. (For more information on this subject, refer to the book list.) Their quilting was meticulous and that in itself formed a great part of each quilt. I also seemed to be drawn towards the patchwork quilts that were 'pieced' together (meaning that the pieces of fabric were sewn together by a seam), rather than those that were appliquéd or applied work. I liked the idea of the straight line forming a limitation to the design of the quilt. So I decided to design my quilts mostly around this technique.

The next thing to do seemed to be to design my own patchwork blocks rather than always using American traditional designs. At first I kept to blocks then started to think of larger areas and treat them as one large block with different shapes throughout the area.

My design inspiration comes from many different sources. I always derive great inspiration from our lovely museums and have good times drawing from their collections. Many of my ideas also come from nature and natural-history books.

I have tried to compile this book by showing how I began making patchwork quilts myself; beginning by experimenting with traditional American patchwork designs and then leading on to more complicated designs of my own. I would like to stress that in my approach there are no hard and fast rules to the craft of patchwork quilting—I am simply putting forward my own preferences in technique. Remember that everyone works in different ways, so experiment and find the way that suits you best.

I hope that there is something here to appeal to both the beginner and the more advanced reader; to give perhaps a few more ideas and inspiration with your future work. Basically it is just a question of joining one piece of fabric to the next, and building up from there. So please go ahead and experiment, and prepare for many hours of work but an awful lot of enjoyment too!

Note:
The measurements used throughout the book are given in both metres and yards. The inch measurements are shown in brackets after the metric measurement. The two measurements do not always correlate, but are chosen in terms of simplifying the unit. Therefore when following these instructions please keep to one type of measurement throughout the instructions.

1. NECESSARY EQUIPMENT

There is not too much involved in collecting together the necessary equipment for making patchwork quilts. I suppose the most important thing is a sewing machine. However there are many hundreds of patchwork quilts made entirely by hand, indeed some people prefer hand sewing. If this is the case your equipment is brought almost right down to the basic needle and thread and a good selection of scrap fabrics. Patchwork is also a craft that doesn't call for an enormous amount of space, and can be carried out quite easily within your living space.

I shall now list in turn the equipment that I feel is important and have found necessary when making my patchwork quilts.

The sewing machine
For me, this has been a really essential piece of equipment and I would not have been able to produce so many quilts without it. A lot of people ask, when they see my patchwork—'Is it sewn by hand or machine?' Well I always do anything that is possible by machine. It is much less time consuming. I see no point in hand sewing just for the sake of it. The machine has been invented, so why not use it? Of course if you do prefer to sew by hand and maybe find it more relaxing, the choice is entirely up to you.

You need a machine that makes a good straight stitch and, if possible, one that will back stitch—to enable you to finish off the thread at the beginning and end of each seam. The choice of machine is entirely up to the individual, everyone has his or her own preferences, whether it is grandma's old treadle or a brand new machine that has twenty different stitches.

Iron
This is also very high on my list of essentials. I find it a great advantage to have a steam iron, as it presses the seams much flatter. It is a good idea to have it permanently set up, fairly near your sewing machine, as it has to be used continually in between sewing each seam.

Scissors

Three pairs are needed. A small nail scissor type to be used for cutting cotton thread and for detailed work such as clipping fabric. The second pair should be a very sharp and good sized pair of cutting out shears, for cutting out the actual fabric. These should be kept as sharp as possible to ensure accurate cutting. It is a good idea to have them sharpened fairly regularly. The third pair are general purpose scissors needed for cutting card and paper etc.

General sewing equipment

A good selection of hand sewing needles is necessary together with tape measure and a general selection of threads and dress pins. I find that the glass headed dress pins are the most useful type, as they are pushed through bulky thicknesses easily without injuring your fingers!

Card and graph paper

You will need a few sheets of graph paper to use for planning your designs and also to make your templates. Thin ticket card is also needed for making the templates.

General drawing equipment

Pencils, crayons, chalk pencils, a rubber, ruler and set square are needed. A set of coloured crayons or felt tip pens will help when designing your quilt. A fairly dark lead pencil to draw on to light fabric and a white crayon or chalk pencil to draw on to dark fabric are also essential.

Dyes

There are many fabrics available from the shops in a wide range of colours. However, I still choose to dye my own fabric. A fair amount of equipment is needed for this but I will give full details in chapter 10, which is devoted entirely to dying fabric.

Choice of materials
Fabric

The choice of your fabric is very personal, everyone having his or her own preferences. It is a good idea to have a large chest in which to save all your types of fabric that you personally like, and every now and then spread them around the floor and pick and choose a new variation of colours and patterns. I have a personal preference for plain colours as I feel that they are more direct in showing up the design and piecing work on the patchwork, but please don't let this stop you from choosing some of the many printed and patterned fabrics available in the stores. I think it is advisable to use an all cotton fabric whenever it is possible. It is much easier to handle when sewing, and also the seams press flatter when ironed. For cutting out, too, it seems not to slide away from the scissors like so many of the synthetic fabrics.

Thread

The type of thread that I recommend for general use in piecing the patchwork is a No. 60 cotton thread, which is slightly finer than the normal sewing thread. I choose the No. 60 thread mainly because it creates less bulk in the seams and where there are many seams, often very close together and overlapping, it helps to keep down the bulk. There also seems to be a much larger colour range available in this type of cotton thread.

When using a certain technique known as 'knotting' or 'tying', which will be described in chapter 2, a cotton crochet thread is good.

Wadding

The type of wadding that I prefer to use is cotton wadding, for several reasons. It will keep the fibre content throughout the whole quilt uniform. When using 100% cotton fabric, it seems natural to use cotton wadding. Also it has quite a lot of weight which allows the finished patchwork quilts to drape well over the corners of the bed or hang flatter when placed on a wall. I also find it a little easier to use than synthetic wadding with my technique of quilting, which I do by machine. Cotton wadding is less spongy than the synthetic type and therefore flows more easily under the machine foot. There is only one problem when using cotton wadding. Unless you quilt it at very regular intervals, it has to be dry cleaned. But providing there is a fairly intense network of quilting it can be washed quite successfully.

Alternatively, Terylene or Courtelle wadding can be used. These are completely washable and need not be quilted as much as the cotton wadding. They are also much lighter in weight, which makes them easier to handle when struggling with the making of the whole quilt. This type of wadding is ideal when using the technique of 'knotting' or 'tying'.

Preparing fabric for your quilt

Just a word here about precautions to take before actually beginning your quilt. A lot of fabrics on the market are not completely dye fast, and many of them contain dressings of various types. It is wise, before beginning to cut into the fabric, to boil it up in detergent to test fastness. This is just to be on the safe side, as it would be terrible to put a great deal of work into a quilt only to find to your horror, that all the colours ran into each other. You may find that while in the process of boiling your fabric, quite a lot of dye may come out into the water. If the amount seems to be excessive, it is not wise to use it at all. But with most types of fabric an initial amount of loose dye may be removed in this manner. Rinse the fabric in warm water until the rinsing water is completely clear. Then dry it in the usual way and iron when slightly damp, before the creases get too set in the fabric.

2. GENERAL SEWING TECHNIQUES

In order to demonstrate the processes involved in making a patchwork quilt, I shall take as an example a very simple traditional American patchwork block called 'pinwheel'.

Having chosen this design, the next step is to decide what size to make it. For this example the finished block will be 20 cm [or 8 in] across. The next move is to draw this block up to the finished scale on graph paper. It is much easier to use graph paper as it ensures that accurate right angles are made.

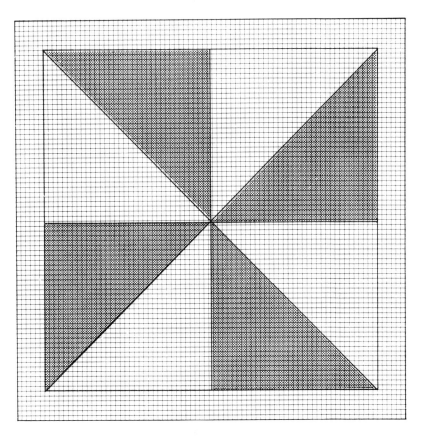

Fig. 1 *'Pinwheel' block*

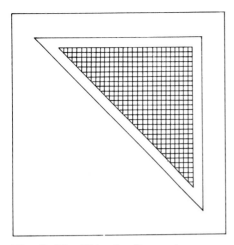

Fig. 2 *The 'Pinwheel' template*

It also saves measuring the lines. Looking at the 'pinwheel' block, it is apparent that there are eight triangles making up the square, and that they are all of the same size. Therefore only one template is needed. Cut one of these triangles out and paste it down to a sheet of ticket card. Now a seam allowance needs to be added to the triangle, so measure 6 mm [or $\frac{1}{4}$ in] out from the edge of the graph paper and rule in the lines on all three sides. Then cut out the template on these lines. Another advantage of having the graph paper gummed on to the template is that it gives an indication of the straight grain of the fabric. When cutting the pieces of fabric out, try to keep the grain of the fabric to the straight lines on the graph paper. In this way the grain will be kept uniform throughout the whole quilt, which helps it to hang well when completed.

Referring back to fig. 1, note that four triangles in dark fabric and four in light are needed. Choose your fabrics and lay them flat on a table. Place the template on the fabric, matching the grain line to the lines on the graph paper. Hold the card down firmly and draw round the template. Use a soft lead pencil for light fabric and a chalk pencil or light coloured crayon for dark fabric. Then cut these triangles out. It is important to be accurate at this stage, because if the fabric is cut out incorrectly, it means that it will be incorrectly sewn together.

Fig. 3 *Drawing around the template*

10

The next step is to join the pieces together. I have allowed 6 mm [or ¼ in] seam allowance on the pieces because the half width of my sewing machine foot (i.e. the distance between the needle and the side of the foot.) measures exactly 6 mm [or ¼ in]. Therefore when sewing these pieces together, all I have to do is match the raw edges of the fabric to the edge of the machine foot and this automatically gives a 6 mm [or ¼ in] seam. If your machine foot is narrower than this, place a piece of sticky tape on the base of your sewing machine, to mark 6 mm [or ¼ in] distance from the needle. Match the raw edges to this when sewing.

It is best to pin the seams together first, then machine along the seam lines, making three or four back stitches at the beginning and end of every seam, to fasten off the ends securely.

Fig. 4 *Sewing the seams by machine*

Fig. 5 *Hand sewing the seams*

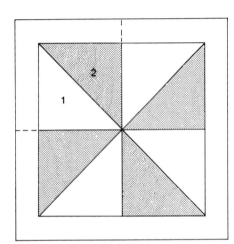

Fig. 6a *Constructing the 'Pinwheel'*

The seams can also be sewn by hand. Some people prefer to hand sew and others may not have the use of a sewing machine. In this case pin the fabrics together as before, with right sides together, and with a needle and thread sew a row of small running stitches, as shown in fig. 5.

Pressing the seams

With my own technique I always press the seams open. It helps to keep the seam lines flat and is also an advantage when quilting by machine at a later stage. However, this is against all tradition, it is usually said that you should press both seams to one side. I would say that if you are sewing the seams by hand, you should use this method as it will make the seams stronger, but when sewing by machine just choose whichever you prefer. Try out a few samples and see which suits you the best. Anyway, the seams must be pressed, which ever way you decide to do it!

This particular 'pinwheel' block is basically made up of four squares, each square being made of two triangles, as illustrated in fig. 6a. Continue by sewing four dark triangles to four light triangles. Then press the seams. You now have four squares which are then sewn together in two pairs. Make sure the shading is correct in each square, to form the 'pinwheel' pattern. Press the seams again.

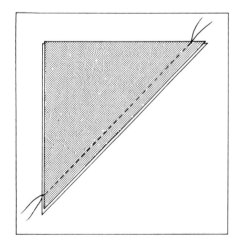

Fig. 6b *Sewing the 'Pinwheel'*

12

Place the two rectangles together, matching the seams by placing pins in at a right angle to the seam, slipping the pin exactly through the two seams that need to be matched, as shown in fig. 7. In this particular block make sure that the points also match by slipping the pin right through the two points which should be 6 mm [or ¼ in] down from the raw edges. Sew along the seam and press. The block is now complete. If you make several blocks and experiment with the colour, you can achieve some very interesting results. In order to help you do this, I have prepared a layout line drawing of the pinwheel block. You can either photocopy this and colour the copy, or place a piece of tracing paper over the top of the drawing and apply the colour on this surface.

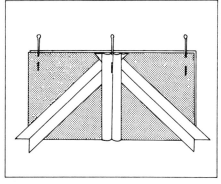

Fig. 7 *Matching the seams*

Quilting

The idea of the quilting is to hold all three layers together and to keep the wadding in place when it goes through the wash. It also makes the patchwork far more substantial and enhances the design of the piecing.

There are several different ways of approaching quilting. I shall attempt to describe three alternative methods, and leave it up to you to decide which suits you best.

Machine quilting

I use this particular method for all of my quilts. Machine quilting seems to be against the tradition of quilt making, but I choose it for speed as it allows me to further my ideas at a faster rate than hand quilting.

To prepare for the quilting, cut a plain piece of cotton fabric a little larger than the piece to be quilted. Cut the wadding to the same size as this backing fabric. Place the wadding over the backing fabric and smooth out gently, making sure not to ruckle the under fabric. Then place the pieced fabric on top of the wadding, and smooth it out, so that there is a 'sandwich' of fabric and wadding. See fig. 8 overleaf.

When all three layers are in place, use pins to secure them and tack the layers together fairly thoroughly. The work is now ready for the machine quilting. Choose a machine foot that doesn't push or bunch the fabric up in front, and where it is possible to see the seam line over which you are stitching. I have a plain sewing foot which seems to be ideal.

Fig. 8 *Laying up the materials for quilting*

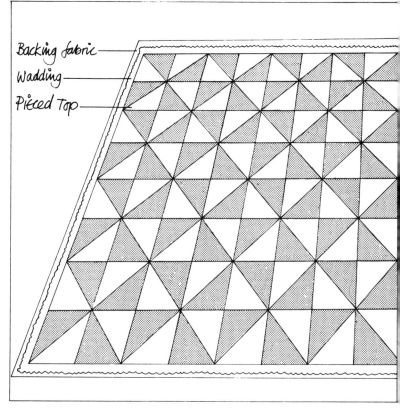

Backing fabric —
Wadding —
Pieced Top —

Because I find it more pleasing to the eye not to see the machine quilting on the top surface of the quilt, I have devised a method of quilting that allows the machine stitching to run along the pieced seam lines thereby sinking hopefully out of sight. See fig. 9.

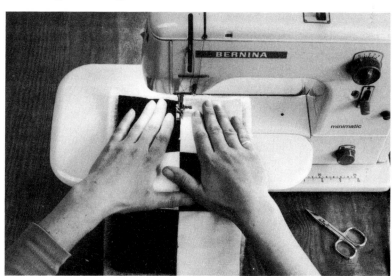

Fig. 9 *Sink stitching for machine quilting*

14

Begin quilting—it takes a bit of practice to keep the stitching exactly in the seam line. Hold your hands firmly either side of the machine foot, keeping the fabric taut and opening up the seam line to its fullest extent to allow the machine stitches to sink down into this groove. If you are going to quilt in small areas, without leaving large spaces unquilted, use cotton wadding as it lies flatter and there is less chance of the top pieced fabric ruckling in front of the machine foot. If using the synthetic wadding, make sure you get a thin 2 oz grade as it would be much more difficult to pass the machine foot over more fluffy wadding and inevitably, it would cause a lot of problems.

After completing the machine quilting, many thread ends are left, which need to be fastened off. Pull them all through to the back. Thread a large-eyed needle with the two threads that are at the beginning and end of each row of stitching. Make a back stitch with them and then feed the needle through under the backing cloth, running it along inside where the wadding lies, for about 2 or 3 cm. Bring the needle back up through the backing fabric and cut off the ends. See fig. 10.

Hand quilting
This is the traditional method of joining the three layers together and is an art in itself. Many old quilts have a terrific amount of hand quilting in them, showing many individual and intricate quilting patterns.

Quilting in your lap
Lay up the three layers as described earlier, and tack very

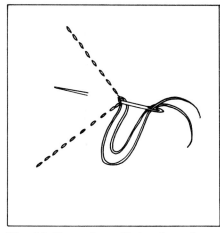

Fig. 10 *Fastening off the threads (for machine quilting)*

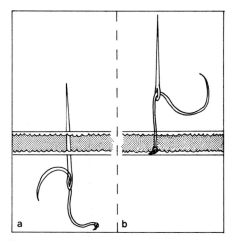

Fig. 11 *Starting the quilting thread*
  a Pushing the needle through the three layers of material
  b Slipping the knot through the backing fabric

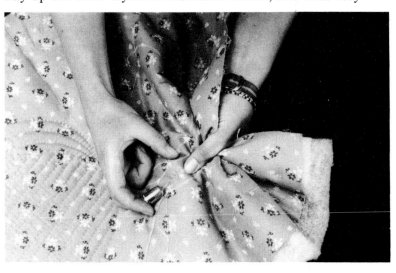

Fig. 12 *Hand quilting without a frame or hoop*

15

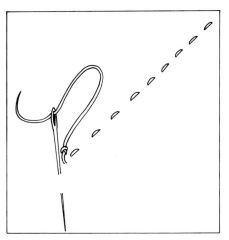

Fig. 13 *Finishing off the thread (for hand quilting)*

thoroughly, keeping all layers firmly in position. This method needs extra tacking as it will be handled much more than the other methods. To quilt by hand use either ordinary cotton thread (No. 40) or special quilting thread, which is quite a bit thicker and stronger than the average thread. Thread a length of cotton on to the needle, tie a small knot in the end and feed the needle up from the bottom, through all three layers. Tug the knot a little to make it pass through the backing fabric, but making sure it doesn't come through to the top surface. Then begin the quilting stitch. Basically this is a small running stitch, which is designed to hold all three layers together. Each stitch should pass through all three layers. The stitches should be of equal length on both the front and back of the work. Pick up about three or four stitches on the needle, then draw them through. Hold your left hand underneath the quilt to feel that the needle has passed right through to the back. See fig. 12. If you find it difficult to achieve an even stitch it may be easier, at first, to take just one stitch at a time until your own technique is developed as shown in fig. 12. This method is used by Michael James and described well in his book 'The Quiltmaker's Handbook'. Here he chooses to wear two thimbles; one to push the needle on top of the quilt and one underneath the quilt (to rebound the needle).

To finish off the end of the cotton, tie a knot very close to the last stitch. Take the needle back through all three layers and tug the knot down, through the layer of fabric, so that it lays inside with the wadding. Then feed the needle along for about 3 cm running it in with the wadding. Pass the needle and thread back out through the top surface again and cut off the thread. Alternatively, finish off with a couple of small back stitches.

Quilting on a frame
Many people who quilt by hand always use a quilting frame. These can be bought (see addresses at the back), or made fairly simply out of four strips of wood.

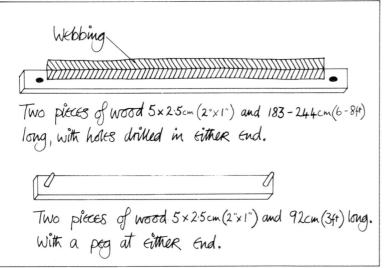

Fig. 14 *The wood needed for a quilting frame*

Webbing

Two pieces of wood 5×2·5cm (2"×1") and 183–244cm (6–8ft) long, with holes drilled in either end.

Two pieces of wood 5×2·5cm (2"×1") and 92cm (3ft) long. With a peg at either end.

Tack or staple a piece of webbing all the way along one side of each of the longer pieces of wood. This is to tack your material and wadding to.

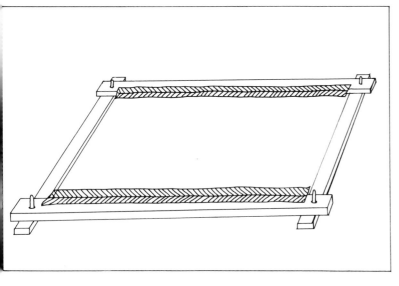

Fig. 15 *Setting the frame up*

Prepare your quilt in the same way as before, laying up all three layers and pinning and tacking them together. Sew one side to the webbing attached to one of the long poles with large tacking stitches. Once this is secure, roll the quilt up around this pole until the width that is left is the right size to join on to the webbing of the opposite long pole, and pulling it fairly taut, tack this side to the webbing on the pole, as shown in fig. 16.

Fig. 16a *Stretching the quilt on the frame*

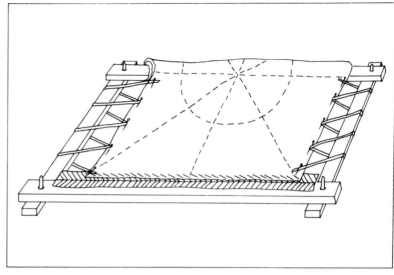

Fig. 16b *Cross-section through the quilting frame, showing how it folds around the poles*

To stretch the sides running parallel to the short poles, use 1 cm [or ⅜ in] wide tape and either pin or tack this tape to the edges of the quilt and pass it around the short poles of the frame, as shown in fig. 16a, stretching it width ways. This frame can be placed on four kitchen-type chairs and the quilting can be started.

The basic stitch and method is identical to that described previously. Keep one hand underneath the frame and make the running stitch from the top. Wear a thimble on the middle finger of your right hand above the frame, in order to push the needle along. Some people find it an advantage to wear some form of protection on their left hand (or the hand underneath the frame) also, as it is often under attack from the needle! Some people just suffer, others wear a leather type of thimble, some wrap a piece of masking tape around their finger and others wear a second thimble. Again choose your own method.

Having quilted the area that is stretched on the frame, roll this quilted section on to the long pole nearest you and unroll the quilt from the other large pole. This now reveals a new area to quilt. Proceed in this manner until the whole quilt is stitched.

Quilting with a quilting hoop

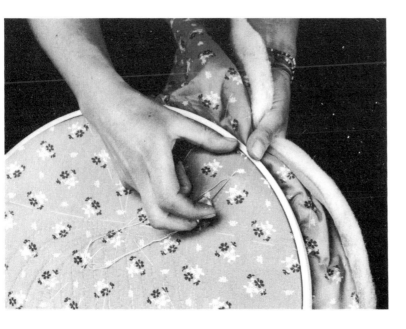

A third method of hand quilting uses a quilting hoop (as illustrated above). This is a most satisfactory method, as the hoop is very easy to handle, it sits comfortably on your lap or a table, and is very easy to store. You can quilt at a moment's notice, without having to set up any large equipment.

When using the hoop, the quilt will need to be tacked together very thoroughly to prevent the fabric layers moving when you change the position of the hoop.

The quilting hoop works on the same principle as the traditional embroidery hoop; the smaller hoop is placed underneath the quilt and the larger hoop placed over it, stretching the fabric. Before starting the quilting stitches, make sure that there is a little 'give' in the fabric. Begin quilting in the centre of the quilt and work towards the outer edges, moving the hoop around as necessary. To quilt the outer edges and corners tack a piece of calico to the outer edges of the quilt. This gives the hoop sufficient fabric to hold as the quilting is finished.

All these methods of hand quilting need quite a lot of practice to achieve an even stitch.

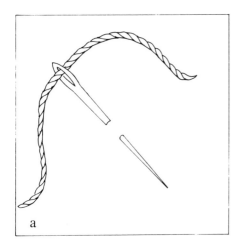

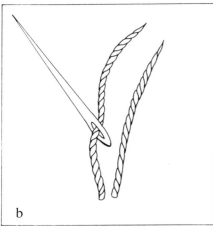

Fig. 17a
Fig. 17b *'Knotting' or 'Tying'*

Knotting or tying

If these techniques of quilting seem too time-consuming, there is an alternative method of joining the three layers of the quilt together. It is known as knotting or tying.

In this case the synthetic wadding must be used as the cotton wadding would probably not hold together after several washes. Begin by laying down the backing fabric, with the wadding next, and finally the pieced work on the top. Proceed as before by pinning and tacking these layers together.

Thread a large needle with crochet cotton. Decide the point at which you want the knot and pass the threaded needle down from the top and back again, about 6 mm [or ¼ in] away from the inserted point, as shown in fig. 17a.

Take special care to pass the needle right through to the backing fabric, making sure that it picks up all three layers of fabric. Next, pull the thread through and remove the needle, so that the two ends of thread are left. Tie these ends together in a reef knot (right over left and left over right) just to make sure that the knot doesn't slip, once tied. Cut the ends of the thread about 3 cm [or 1¼ in] away from the knot.

This method leaves the knots of the crochet cotton on the top of the quilt. This is a traditional method and the idea is to allow these knots to form a part of the design of the quilt. It's up to you where you place them on your quilt. A distance of about 10 cm [or 4 in] between each knot is a pretty good guide, but of course it will depend a lot on your design. If you don't want the tied ends to show, it is quite in order to reverse the knot and have it on the back of the quilt, so that the front would barely show any sign of it.

To finish the quilt edges

At this stage the whole of the pieced work is quilted.

I use three alternative methods for finishing off the edges on a quilt.
1 Framing the quilt.
2 Binding with straight strips.
3 Binding with bias strips.

Framing the quilt

Make a paper pattern for the quilt fabric frame. Draw two parallel lines the required width of the framing piece. Measure the length of the quilt edges and mark this measurement on one of the drawn lines. Then make a 45° angle to the opposite edge, as shown in fig. 18. Mark in a 6 mm [or ¼ in] seam allowance around all sides.

Cut out 8 of this shape, and use them to construct 2 frames. When joining the corners, leave the last 6 mm [or ¼ in] of the seam on the inner corner unsewn, as shown in fig. 19. This is to make the manipulation easier when sewing the corner to the pieced section.

Pin one frame in position around the pieced work (Fig. 20). Then tack and machine. When you reach the corners and have sewn right up to the seam line, keep the needle down in the fabric and lift the foot. Re-arrange the fabric and swivel the whole quilt around, replace the foot and start sewing in the new direction of the next edge (See fig. 21).

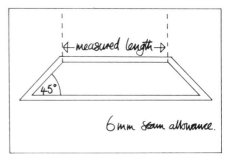

Fig. 18 *Making the template pattern for the frame*

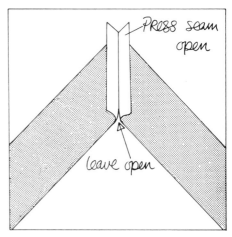

Fig. 19 *Sewing the angled corner seams*

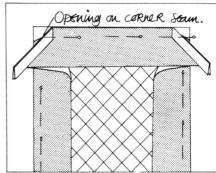

Fig. 20 *Setting the frame in position*

Fig. 21 *Turning the corners*

21

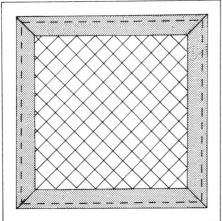

Fig. 22 *Sewing on the second frame to finish off the edges*

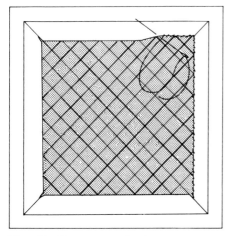

Fig. 23 *Hemming the frame*

Fig. 24 *Cutting off the surplus wadding*

When this has been completed, pin the second frame into position, with right sides facing. Tack and machine around all sides (Fig. 22). Clip the surplus wadding off the corners. Turn this frame to the back, and poke out the corners. Turn in the 6 mm [or ¼ in] seam allowance and hem around the edges, as shown in fig. 23.

Binding with straight strips

For this method there must be a surplus of backing and wadding allowed around all edges. About 3 cm [or 1¼ in].

Measure the length of two opposite sides of the quilt, and cut two pieces this length and about 7 cm [or 3 in] wide. Place one strip on each side of the quilt, right sides together, and sew them on using the usual 6 mm [or ¼ in] for the seam allowance. From this stitching line, measure 2.50 cm [or 1 in] and trim the surplus wadding at this point (See fig. 24).

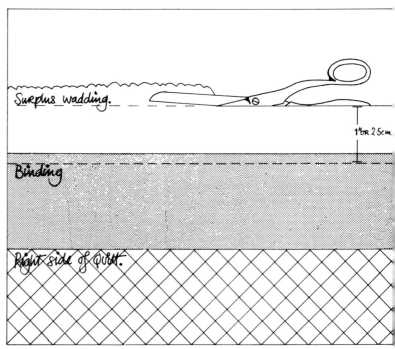

old the binding over the wadding, tuck in the seam llowance and hem stitch on the back (See fig. 25).

Fig. 25 *Hemming the back of the straight strip binding*

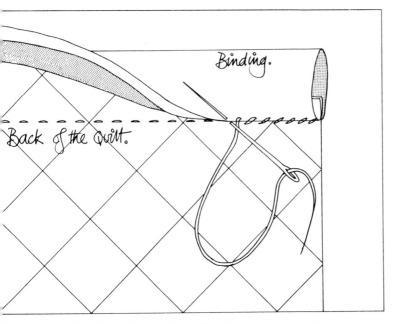

ut the required length bindings for the two opposite edges, his time adding a 6 mm [or ¼ in] seam allowance on each nd. Sew these bindings in position and finish off, as shown in g. 26. Hand sew the corners and the back edges.

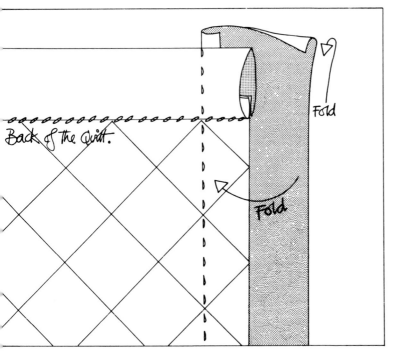

Fig. 26 *Binding the corners, using straight strips*

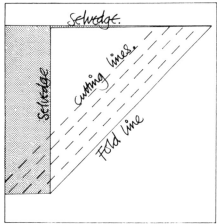

Fig. 27 *How to cut bias strips*

Binding with bias strips

For this method, measure the perimeter of the quilt, and prepare one long length of bias strip, a little longer than this measurement, by cutting several bias strips 6 cm [or $2\frac{1}{4}$ in] wide and joining them together, as shown in figs. 27 and 28.

Press the seams. Press the whole length of the bias strip in half so that it now measures 3 cm [or $1\frac{1}{8}$ in] in width. There are now two raw edges on one side and a fold on the other. Place the raw edge side against the raw edges of the quilt on the right side. Sew into position, taking a 6 mm [or $\frac{1}{4}$ in] seam allowance. When you reach the corners, clip into the binding to allow it to turn the corner easily (See fig. 29). Then continue to sew along the next edge. Sew the binding around all sides and join. Turn the bias over the raw edges to the back and hem (See fig. 30).

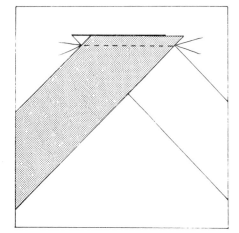

Fig. 28 *Joining the bias strips*

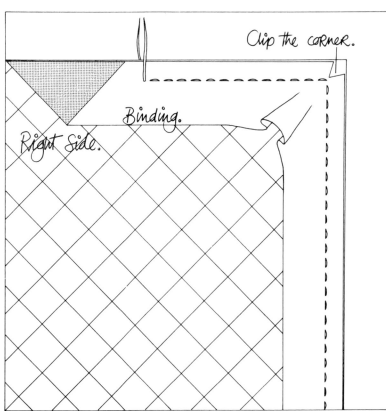

Fig. 29 *Sewing on the bias binding*

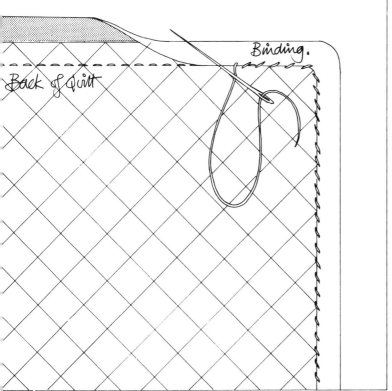

Fig. 30 *Hemming the binding*

Hanging the quilt

Although many of the quilts described are to be used on beds, it is also nice to be able to hang them on the wall. For this reason I always sew a cloth channel to the top reverse side of the quilt. This is to accommodate a wooden rod or pole from which the quilt can be hung.

Cut a strip of fabric the required length of your quilt, and about 15 cm [or 6 in] wide. Fold it in half, length ways and sew 1.5 cm [or ½ in] seams on either end (See fig. 31). Bag this out, so that you have three finished edges and one with raw edges. Insert the raw edged side into the binding along the top edge of the quilt. Hand sew the folded edge to the back of the quilt and leave the two short edges open to accommodate the wooden pole.

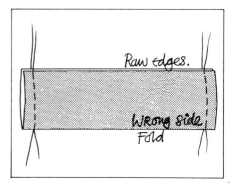

Fig. 31 *Making the cloth channel for hanging the quilt*

25

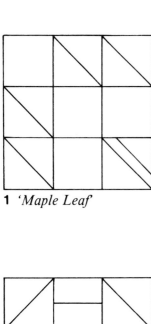

1 *'Maple Leaf'*

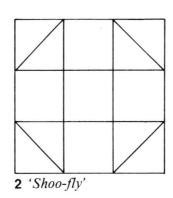

2 *'Shoo-fly'*

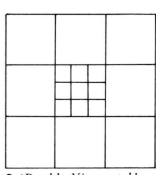

3 *'Double Nine-patch'*

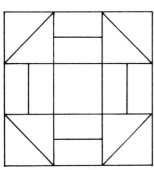

4 *'Churn Dash'*

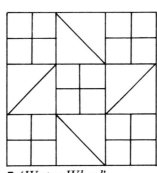

5 *'Water Wheel'*

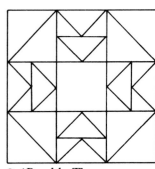

6 *'Double T'*

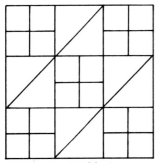

7 *'Jacobs Ladder'*

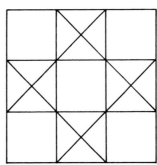

8 *'Variable Star'*

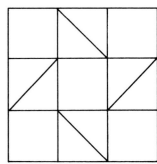

9 *'Friendship Star'*

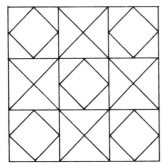 **10** *'Blocks and Stars'*

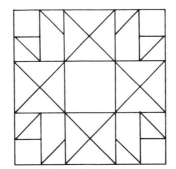 **11** *'Union Stone'*

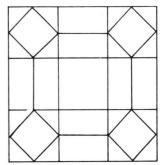 **12** *'Rolling Stone'*

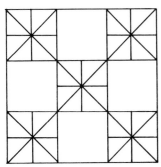 **13** *'Pinwheels'*

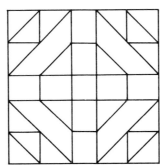 **14** *'Wedding Rings'*

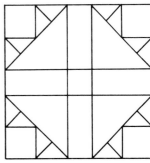 **15** *'Cross and Crown'*

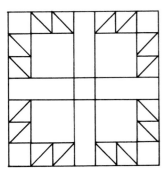 **16** *'Bears Paw'*

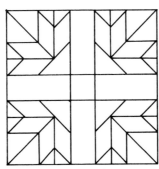 **17** *'Goose Tracks'*

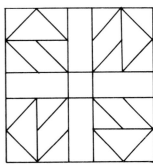 **18** *'Jack-in-the-box'*

27

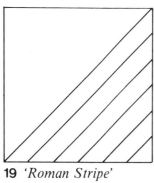

19 *'Roman Stripe'*

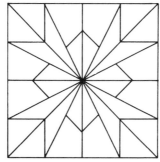

20 *'St. Louis Star'*

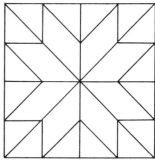

21 *'Eight pointed Star'*

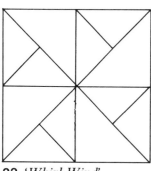

22 *'Whirl Wind'*

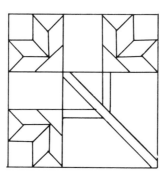

23 *'Noon-day Lily'*

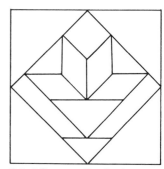

24 *'Cactus Basket'*

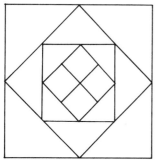

25 *'Monkey Wrench'*

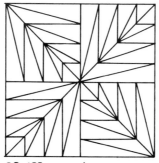

26 *'Hosanna'*

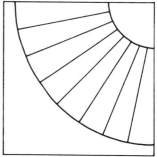

27 *'Grandmothers Fan'*

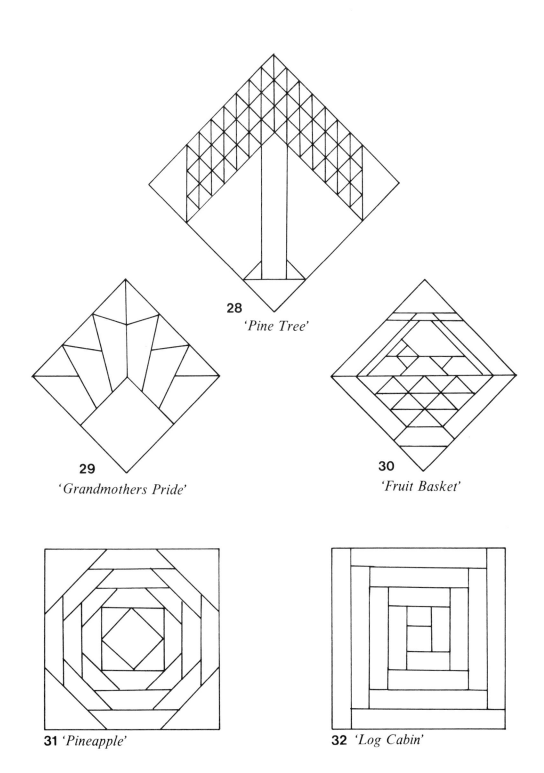

28 *'Pine Tree'*

29 *'Grandmothers Pride'*

30 *'Fruit Basket'*

31 *'Pineapple'*

32 *'Log Cabin'*

3. TRADITIONAL AMERICAN BLOCKS

In this chapter, I have chosen a few traditional American block patterns. There are many block designs that have grown along with the history of patchwork. Many women created new designs of their own, and by passing on a block idea to a neighbour or friend, created the tradition of that block. However rigid this idea of using a block design may seem, each block can be used in many different ways. Even if the same block is presented to two different people, you will never have the same result at the end and each quilt will have an individual character of its own. The choice of fabric, the scale of the block, and the different ways in which it can be made up project a new concept of the familiar block.

The idea of the block pattern is fairly simple. Choose a block design which you like, and work out what size you would like to make it, taking into consideration the total size of the quilt you have in mind. Work out how many blocks you need to make for the finished quilt and sew the required number. It is advisable to make one sample block first before cutting the others out, just to make sure the pattern is correct.

One of the most simple traditional patchwork blocks is the 'nine-patch' block. It is made up of nine equal sized squares, and is very easy to construct, by simply sewing the three squares together to form three rows of three patches. Match the seams and sew these three rows together to complete the block. I have deliberately chosen twelve blocks based on this construction, it will make it easier for beginners to work with these ideas.

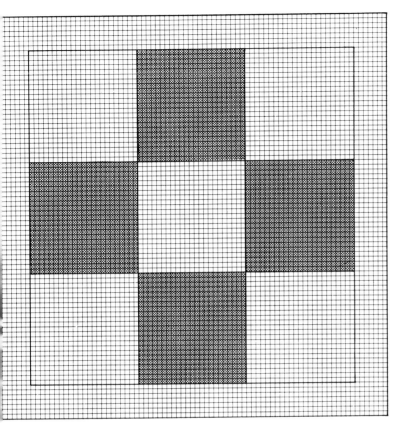

Fig. 32 'Nine-Patch' block

The remaining five blocks are based on a 'nine-patch' block, but instead of having nine equal squares the proportions are changed (See fig. 33). This leaves four large squares, one small square and four oblong units. This block can be constructed in the same way as the normal 'nine-patch'.

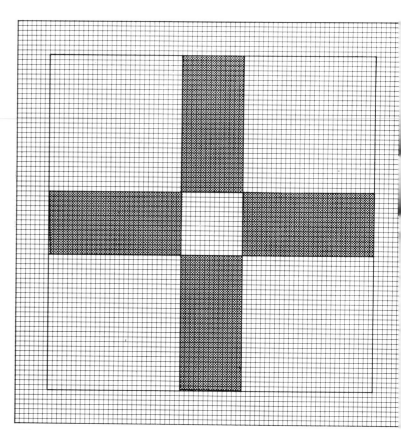

Fig. 33 *Distorted 'nine-patch' block*

The other blocks I have chosen simply because the designs appeal to me. Each one is constructed in a different way. Draw the block on graph paper to the size you require, and make each template needed as described in chapter 2. When constructing each block, you must consider where to start building up the pieces to form larger units and gradually working your way through the block.

When designing your quilt, using the block method, you may decide that a border pattern would sit nicely around the initial blocks, thereby framing them. Quite often a simple plain border can really set off the block design. However, you may wish to use a traditional pattern.

Page 34 shows four suggestions—once again the colour and tone can be varied in many different ways.

Pages 35–47 show layout drawings using repeated block designs. These are to use to experiment with colour. You can either trace off the grid and apply the colour, or place a sheet of tracing paper over the layout drawings and apply the colour directly to the tracing paper. You will be able to work out many variations on each block design.

Border Patterns

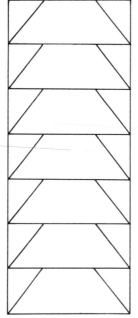

1 *'Tree Everlasting'*

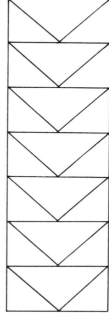

2 *'Wild Goose Chase'*

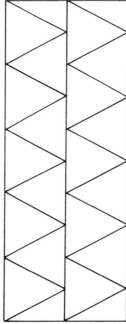

3 *'Streak of Lightning'*

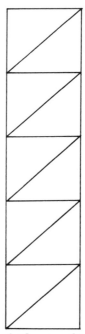

4 *'Sawtooth'*

A. 'Pinwheel'

B. *'Variable Star' (based on the 'nine-patch' block)*

C. 'Water Wheel' (based on the 'nine-patch' block)

D. *Wedding Rings*

38

E. *'Log Cabin'*

F. *'Fruit Basket'*

G. *'Monkey Wrench'* or *'Snails Trail'*

H.   'St. Louis Star'

I. *'Double T' (based on the 'nine-patch' block)*

J. 'Kaleidoscope 1'

44

K. *'Kaleidoscope Variation'*

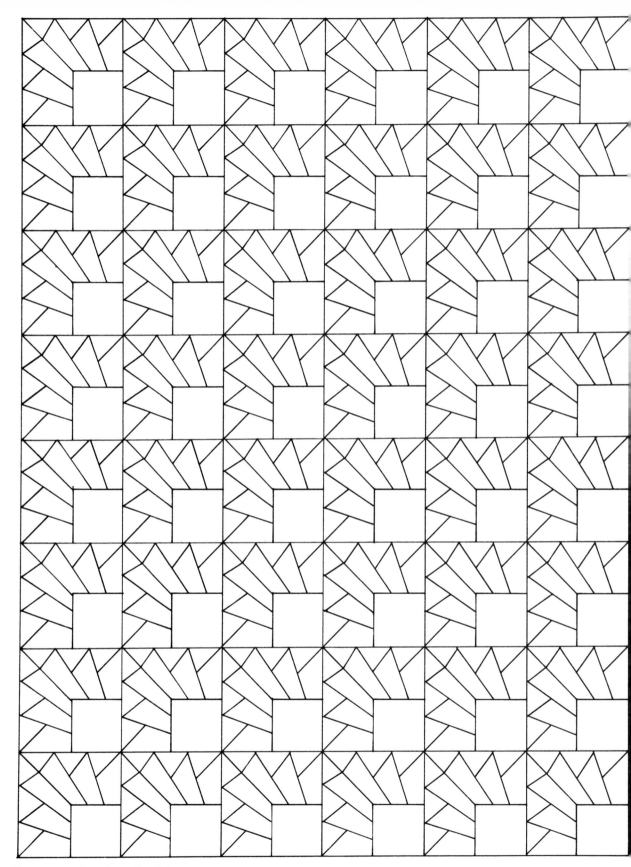

L. *'Grandmothers Pride'*

M. *'Windmill Variation'*

4. PLANNING AND DESIGNING

For something that takes so long to make, it is always worth putting a lot of effort into the planning and designing of your quilt.

Different people have their own way of approaching this. Some people work with drawings first, sometimes sketching in black and white, sometimes planning colour themes. Other people work straight from their fabric collections, perhaps allowing a colour theme to emerge from their scrap boxes. Or perhaps they cut out certain shapes in fabric and pin these shapes on to a board to begin to plan the final design. Some people may also work by making up several blocks and then arranging them and deciding how they would be best put together. Everyone has his or her own methods.

After a little experimental work, you will begin to devise your own system. Personally I find it best to begin by working out a detailed finished drawing. First I have an idea and work on a few rough drawings. I have a personal preference for using piecing rather than appliqué, therefore I need to work out the design mostly within a framework of straight lines, rather than using curves.

My next step, having decided the subject matter, is to draw my design on to graph paper. From this point, I begin to work out the grid of straight lines throughout the design. I usually draw it up to scale, using so many squares to represent a square inch. This makes it easier for me to translate the drawing into a large scale quilt. It gives me a very good idea of the finished image, and I can keep referring to it for the specified shapes and colours planned.

I usually make a line drawing first, to plan the actual shapes and dimensions of the quilt. When I am satisfied with this, I begin to work on the colour. Most of the time I use coloured crayons for this.

Design for Egyptian Scarab Quilt

50

Design for Large Fruit Basket Quilt

Although this may all take some time, the length of time in comparison to making the actual quilt is minimal and I think is worth it. I can look at the drawing critically and decide whether the design and colour works, or if certain parts need to be changed. It is much easier to decide, at this point rather than half way through making the quilt.

The actual design of your quilt can follow many different paths. There are many design sources. Inspiration can come from many things, and if you catch the 'patchwork bug' as I have done, you will be able to see patchwork patterns in almost everything you look at! Many things can trigger off a sudden design idea for a quilt.

Practically thinking, it is probably best to begin with something that is not too complicated or ambitious, just to get the hang of it! To practice the techniques given, it may be a good idea to make up a few sample blocks. Or alternatively, make a few of the given instructions for the various blocks, into cushions. These can be a good starting point, as they are projects that will not take too long.

'Maple leaf' block cushion

Fig. 34 *Design for 'Maple Leaf' cushion*

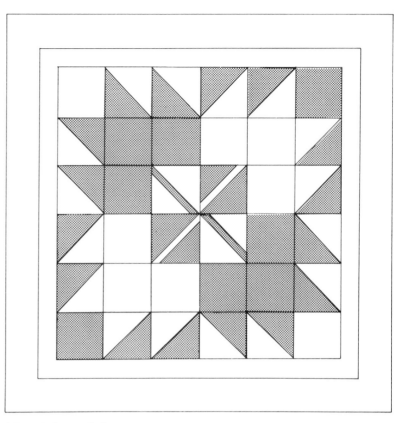

Materials needed

Fabric— Black—1 m [or 1 yd]
White—.25 cm [or ¼ yd]
Backing fabric—.70 cm [or ¾ yd]
Wadding—.70 cm [or ¾ yd]
1-16 in black zip.

Make up four 'Maple leaf' blocks, (as described in chapter 5). Make two with black leaves and two with white leaves. Piece them together as shown in fig. 34.

Make the framing pattern, as shown in fig. 35, and cut eight pieces this size in black fabric.

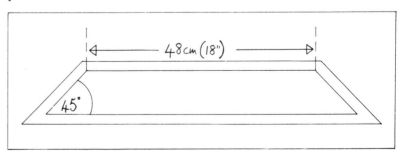

Fig. 35 *Template for the frame of the cushion*

Join them together to make up two frames. Leave the last 6 mm [or ¼ in] on every inside corner unsewn, so that it can be manipulated when sewing on to the central panel. Sew one frame around the 'Maple leaf' blocks (See chapter 2).

After piecing the cushion, it is ready to quilt. I find that this makes the finished cushion more substantial and it also strengthens the pieced fabric. Quilt it using whichever method you prefer, either by hand or machine.

Next, make up the cushion cover. Cut the back of the cushion from one piece of fabric, making it the same size as the quilted top, apart from one edge which needs to be 6 mm [or ¼ in] larger. Fold this same edge over 1.5 cm [or ⅝ in] and press. Sew the zip face down on to one edge of the quilted top. Turn the zip over so that it automatically folds the seam allowance back. Then place the folded edge of the backing fabric over the other half of the zip, so that the teeth are covered. Pin and machine the zip in place.

With right sides facing, place the pieced top and the backing fabric together, and sew around the remaining three edges, catching in the seams immediately either side of the zip. Clip off the bulk of wadding at each corner and then turn the whole cushion cover back to the right side.

Use a separate cushion interior to fill the cushion, making its dimensions approximately 2.5 cm [or 1 in] larger than the finished size of the cover.

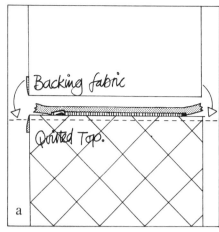

Fig. 36a *Sewing the zip into position*

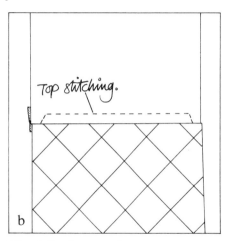

Fig. 36b *Sewing the zip into position*

5. THE 'DAY-LILY' QUILT

This was one of the first patchwork quilts that I made. At this stage I was following the form of traditional American quilt designs, and in this particular quilt, I used two traditional blocks. The 'noon-day lily', and the 'maple leaf'. It is a large double size quilt, measuring 216 cm [or 81 in] × 251 cm [or 96 in].

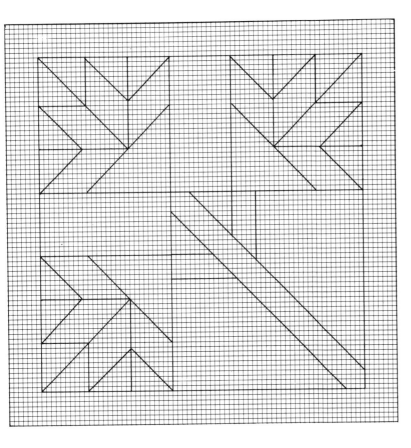

Fig. 37 *'Noon-day Lily' block*

Fig. 38 'Maple Leaf' block

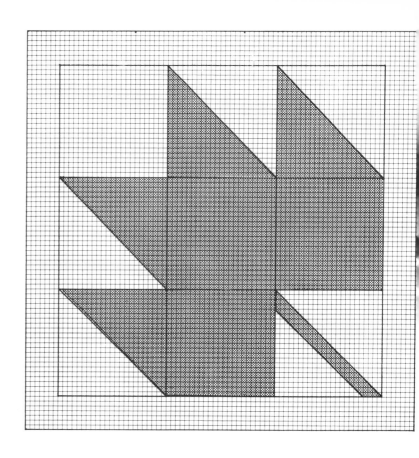

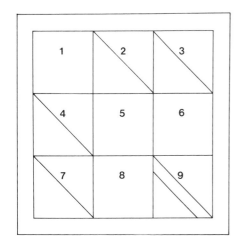

Fig. 39 'Maple Leaf' divided into nine parts

56

Materials needed
All the fabric listed is 36 in wide.
For the pieced top.
Black—5.5 m [or 6 yd]
Blue—3.2 m [or 3½ yd]
Rust—2.4 m [or 2½ yd]
White—2.1 m [or 2¼ yd]
Wadding (36 in wide)—7 m [or 7¾ yd]
Backing fabric—7 m [or 7¾ yd]

Maple leaf block
This block is constructed very simply on the basis of a 'nine-patch' block. If you study it you will see that it breaks up easily into nine patches, as shown in fig. 39.

Four of these patches are squares, and four are made up of two triangles each. The ninth has two triangles and one strip to form the stem.

Draw the 'Maple leaf' block on to graph paper, the actual size of the finished block. When we study this, you can see that only four templates are needed, as shown in fig. 40.

Template 1—Square.
    ,,   2—triangle.
    ,,   3—Smaller triangle.
    ,,   4—Strip for the stem.

Cut these templates shapes out from the drawing and make them in the usual manner (as described in chapter 2).

Next, proceed to cut out the fabric. Cut out the necessary number of each template from the fabric, referring to fig. 40.

You will need to make up 30 blocks in blue and rust, and 14 in black and white. I would advise you to always make up a sample block, just to make sure that your pattern and templates are correct.

Sew all the triangles (template 2) in pairs, one black and one white (or one rust and one blue), and press the seams. Next make up the square with the stem in it, as shown in fig. 41. Always keep to the 6 mm [or ¼ in] seam allowance.

When the nine squares are complete, sew them together in the appropriate order, joining three rows of three squares, then matching the seams to complete the whole block, as shown in fig. 42.

When matching the seams, place the pins at a right angle to the seams. Pass the point of the pin through the two seams that are to be matched and proceed to sew the seam, taking the usual 6 mm [or ¼ in] seam allowance. It is usually all right to sew over the pins, but slow down when approaching them, just to make sure the sewing machine needle does not hit the pin.

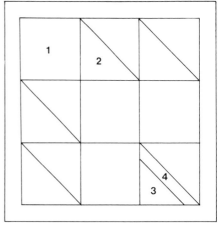

Fig. 40 *The four templates needed*

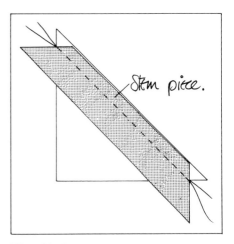

Fig. 41 *Sewing the stem square*

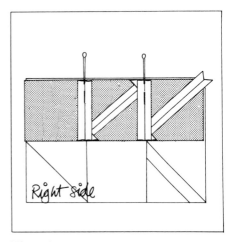

Fig. 42 *Matching the seams*

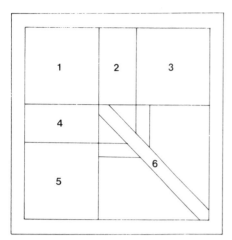

Fig. 43 *Units for making up the 'noon-day lily' block*

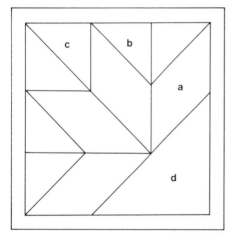

Fig. 44 *Unit 1 templates*

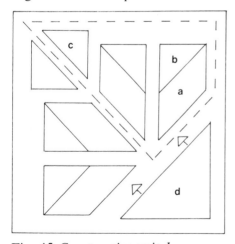

Fig. 45 *Constructing unit 1*

'Noon-day lily' block

The 'noon-day lily' block is slightly more complicated. It is also a traditional pattern, although there are many variations of this block, and often it has an appliquéd stem. I always prefer pieced work, therefore I deliberately pieced the stem in this block.

Draw the block to full size on to graph paper, making the size of the block the same as the 'maple leaf', 24 cm [or 9 in] square. Divide the block into larger units, as shown in fig. 43 and make the templates for these units. You will only need to make the templates for units 1, 2 and 6, as the other units 3, 4 and 5 are just repeats of the former ones.

Unit 1

When drawing up unit 1, make sure you draw it in such a way that the four petals of the lily are of equal size and shape. It's just a matter of getting the proportions correct (See fig. 44). The main reason for doing this, is so that each petal will be identical and therefore there will be no chance of getting them mixed up, or out of order.

Make four templates for unit 1, as shown in fig. 48. Make sure you mark the grain line on the template. Then proceed to cut out the fabric. For the whole block 3 units of the flower head are needed. Refer to fig. 37. Cut 12 of template 'A' in white, for the total block, twelve of template 'C' in blue, and 3 of template 'D' in black fabric.

Sew the various pieces together as shown in fig. 45, first joining the templates 'A' to 'B', then joining the three pieces surrounded by the dotted line, and finally adding the triangular piece 'D'. For each block 3 of this unit are needed.

Unit 2

Make the template for unit 2 (See fig. 43). In this case it is a simple rectangle shape. Make the template in the usual manner. Then cut out two of this template for each block, in blue fabric.

Unit 6

Make the templates for unit 6, a, b, c and d, as shown in fig.
46.

When drawing this up, make sure that the stems meet and
match the flower heads on the block. Make the width of b
and d about 1.5 cm [or ½ in] wide.

Piece a to b and c and then join both sections by piecing in
template d.

Sew and piece each of the units shown in fig. 43, and sew
each unit together to form the finished block.

For the total quilt you need to make up 12 blocks of the
'noon-day lily'. These will make up the central panel.

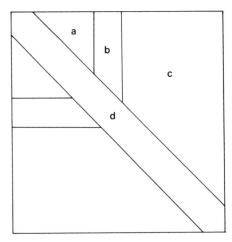

Fig. 46 *Unit 6 templates*

Piecing the blocks together

In my own methods of quilting (described in chapter 2), I use
the machine. Therefore in the case of a large quilt, I find it
necessary to divide it into sections. The 'Day-Lily' quilt can be
divided into 3 sections quite easily as shown in fig. 47.
However, if you wish to quilt by hand, piece the entire quilt
together and stretch it on to a quilting frame or use a hoop
for this purpose (as described in chapter 2).

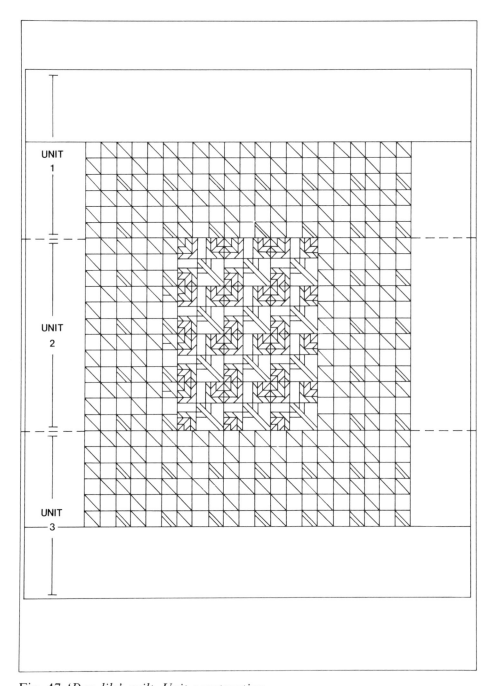

Fig. 47 *'Day-lily' quilt. Unit construction*

The border

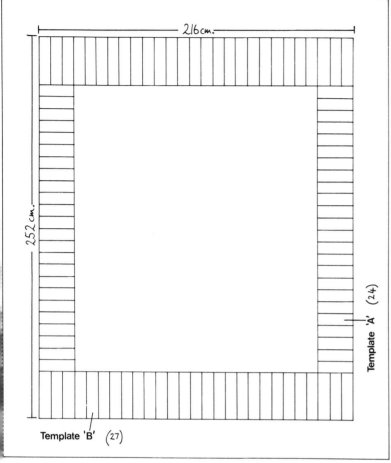

Fig. 48 *The border*

Although the black border is all of one colour, I have deliberately made it out of strips that measure 8 cm [or 3 in] in width. This is to accommodate the quilting. For the border make two rectangular templates, measuring:

A—8 cm [or 3 in] × 24 cm [or 9 in].
B—8 cm [or 3 in] × 30 cm [or 12 in].

Add the usual 6 mm [or ¼ in] seam allowance to these measurements. Cut out 48 of template 'A' and 54 of template 'B', for the entire border.

61

Treat the whole quilt in three separate units as labeled in fig. 47.

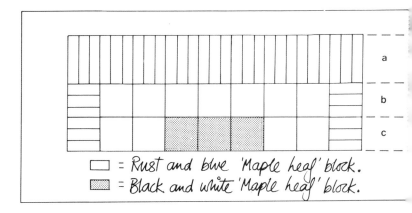

Fig. 49 *Unit 1—constructing the blocks*

Piecing quilt unit 1

Divide unit 1 into 3 long strips, as labeled in fig. 49 a, b and c.

a. Piece together 27 of template 'B' of the border.

b. Sew 7 of the rust and blue 'Maple Leaf' blocks together. Then join six of template 'A' of the border, and sew three of each of these on to each end of the 'Maple leaf'.

c. Sew three black and white 'Maple leaf' blocks together. Add two rust and blue blocks to each end. Next sew the black border pieces on either end.

Sew all three sections together to form the total unit 1. Make sure to match all the seams.

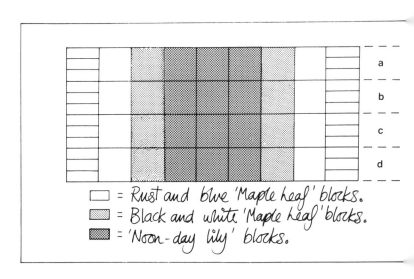

Fig. 50 *Unit 2—constructing the blocks*

62

Piecing quilt unit 2

Divide this unit into 4 identical rows (See fig. 50).

To piece each row begin in the centre by piecing together 3 blocks of the 'day lily'. Then add one black and white 'maple leaf', followed by one rust and blue 'maple leaf' to each end. Finally add the border pieces, and sew the 4 rows together, as shown in fig. 50.

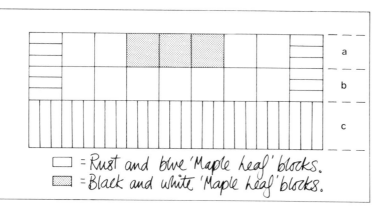

☐ = Rust and blue 'Maple Leaf' blocks.
▨ = Black and white 'Maple Leaf' blocks.

Fig. 51 *Unit 3—constructing the blocks*

Piecing quilt unit 3

Again divide this unit into 3 rows a, b and c. Piece each together, referring to fig. 51.

Quilting the sections

The next stage is to quilt each of these sections.

Cut 3 lengths of 36 in wide fabric 2.3 m [or 2¾ yd] long, allowing plenty of extra backing and wadding on the outside edges. Lay the back flat on to a large table, and smooth out the wadding on the top of it. Finally lay the pieced work over this, and continue as described in chapter 2.

Finishing off

Join all three units together and finish using the straight strip binding method given in chapter 2.

6. 'KORKY THE CAT' QUILT

The idea for this quilt came from looking at picture knitting patterns and needlepoint designs. In this case, one small square unit represented one stitch. In the patchwork, it is represented by one small square of fabric. It seemed a theme with endless possibilities. And indeed, when I came to look back at some historical quilts, this theme had been used and called 'postage stamp' quilts. There were fine examples which exploited this theme, and made pictures emerge from the squares.

I made 'Korky' to use as a curtain, to hang before a collection of childrens' annuals, including some 'Dandy' annuals, with many cartoons of 'Korky' drawn on them. So I thought it would be a nice idea to enlarge this image to use on the quilt. The finished size of the quilt is 252 cm [or 95 in] × 280 cm [or 105 in].

Material needed:

All fabric used is 36 in wide.
Black—6.5 m [or 7 yd]
White—4 m [or 4½ yd]
Red—.75 cm [or ¾ yd]
Black and white stripe—6 m [or 5¾ yd]
Green—1 m [or 1¼ yd]
Backing fabric—9 m [or 9½ yd]
Wadding (36 in wide)—9 m [or 9½ yd]

Draw the image of 'Korky' on to ¼ in graph paper, referring to fig. 52 and transfer each square from this drawing, on to the larger square of your graph paper. You will now have a good size drawing to work from. It is a good idea to colour the drawing lightly to indicate the colour of the fabrics to be used.

The central panel, 'Korky's' head, is made entirely from 4 cm [or 1½ in] squares. So make one template for the whole of the inner quilt.

Fig. 52 *Design for 'Korky the Cat' Quilt*

Fig. 53 *General construction of 'Korky the Cat' quilt*

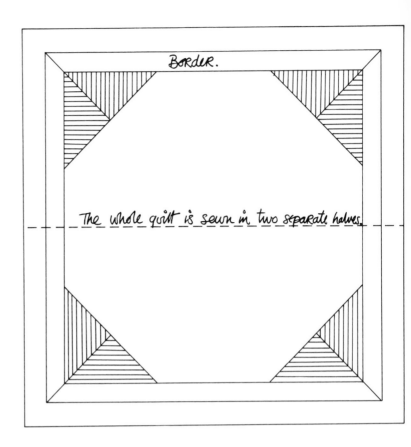

BORDER.

The whole quilt is sewn in two separate halves.

Trace the template from fig. 54 and either make it in fairly thick card, so that the edges will not wear down, or keep checking the size against this drawing, and redraw when necessary. Accuracy is essential in this quilt, as every small error will be duplicated on all the seams.

Begin at the top of the drawing. Count the number of squares needed in each row, and work from row to row. Cut the required number of squares needed, then piece them together in the correct order. Keep referring to your drawing.

Unless you can devise a really foolproof way of cutting through several thicknesses of fabric, do not attempt it. There is a tendency for the fabric to slide as you are cutting it, and you end up with squares that are unequal in size.

Fig. 54 *Template for 'Korky the Cat' quilt—actual size*

66

The **making** process of this quilt is very straight forward. Simply work your way through the rows as they are laid out in the drawing. Each square on the graph paper is equal to one square of fabric. Work in rows across the drawing and every now and then join a few rows together. Match the seams, as shown in fig. 55.

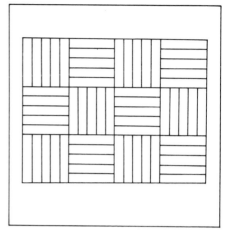

Fig. 56 *Piecing the striped squares*

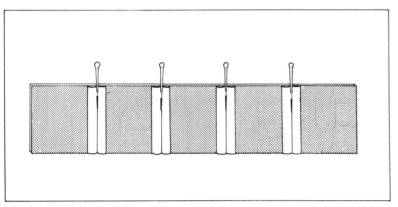

Fig. 55 *Matching the seams*

Place the background squares of striped fabric at alternative angles, having one stripe reading vertically and the other horizontally, as shown in fig. 56.

The whole quilt is pieced in two separate halves, for ease when quilting. Therefore piece the central panel in two halves, as shown in fig. 53.

The corners and the border
For the corner sections you will need to use 2 m [or 2 yd] of the striped fabric. Cut this into triangles, as shown in fig. 57.

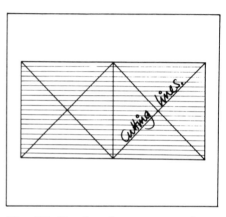

Fig. 57 *Cutting the corner sections*

Rearrange the pairs of triangles so that they form a striped border, as shown in fig. 53. The four corners are not equal. There is ample fabric to accommodate the largest corner, and the other corners can be trimmed down accordingly. Find the central point of each of the unfinished corners, and match the central seam of each of the corner pieces to this. Trim off the surplus amount of fabric, as shown in fig. 58.

Make a framed border in black cloth 10 cm [or 4 in] wide and sew it around the outside edges, keeping the quilt in two separate halves. Use the sewing method previously described in chapter 2, for framing the quilt. Cut a second frame of equal measurements, but this time all in one framed piece. Set this aside for finishing off the edges.

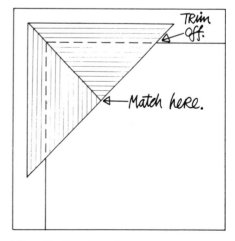

Fig. 58 *Piecing the corners*

To quilt

Prepare the backing fabric by cutting six lengths of 1.5 m [or 1 yd 23 in]. Join three together for the top half of the quilt, and three for the lower half, keeping the quilt in two halves. Lay the wadding over the backing, and finally the pieced sections.

Proceed to quilt. For the central area it is adequate to quilt in the seam lines running horizontally, there is no need to quilt the vertical seams as well.

To quilt the corner sections, run the machine stitching line along the stripes at about 4 or 5 cm [or $1\frac{1}{2}$–2 in] intervals.

Join the two halves of the quilt together, and finish. With right sides together, place the second completed frame on the quilt and sew around all edges. Then bag out the corners and hand sew the inner frame edge to the wrong side of the quilt. Finish as described in chapter 2 to complete the quilt.

The fruit basket wallhanging

An extension of this idea is the 'Fruit Basket' wallhanging. After making 'Korky', using the square as a unit, it seemed the next logical step to use strips instead of joining rows of squares together. Basically the strip is all one piece, until the colour changes, and then there is a seam.

To make up the wallhanging, you still read across in rows, and then join the rows together. I have found that this method is good for representational images, as a fairly high degree of detail can be achieved.

The size of the finished hanging is 122 cm [or 48 in] square.

This time, instead of using blocks, as in most traditional American patchwork, the fruit basket is treated as one large block.

Study the drawing in fig. 59 carefully, and draw it up on a large sheet of graph paper, to the actual size. The width of each strip is 2.5 cm [or 1 in]. On the drawing add numbers as indicated in fig. 62, for your own reference.

Material needed:

(Add the abbreviations in the brackets to your drawing)

Approximate fabric measurements:

Light grey (L.G.)—75 cm [or $\frac{3}{4}$ yd]

Dark grey (D.G.)—75 cm [or $\frac{3}{4}$ yd]

Black (B)—2 m [or $1\frac{3}{4}$ yd]

Rust (R)—50 cm [or $\frac{1}{2}$ yd]

Cream (C)—75 cm [or $\frac{3}{4}$ yd]

Yellow (Y)—50 cm [or $\frac{1}{2}$ yd]

Khaki (K)—2 m [or $1\frac{3}{4}$ yd]

Purple (P)—50 cm [or $\frac{1}{2}$ yd]

Mauve (M)—50 cm [or $\frac{1}{2}$ yd]

Pink (Pi)—50 cm [or $\frac{1}{2}$ yd]

Dark green (D.Gr.)—50 cm [or $\frac{1}{2}$ yd]

Light green (L.Gr.)—50 cm [or $\frac{1}{2}$ yd]

Mid. green (M.Gr.)—25 cm [or $\frac{1}{4}$ yd]

Beige (Bi)—25 cm [or $\frac{1}{4}$ yd]

Brown (Br)—25 cm [or $\frac{1}{4}$ yd]

Backing fabric—2.8 m [or 3 yd]

Wadding (36 in wide)—2.8 m [or 3 yd]

Refer to the central area of the 'Large Fruit Basket Quilt' for colour.

The whole image is worked in 2.5 cm [or 1 in] strips, with the exception of the fruit basket handle; this is made up of three upright shapes.

On studying the whole design you can see that several shapes are repeated throughout. Therefore, pick these out and make templates of the squares and triangles etc. Do this by tracing the shape from the drawing on to a sheet of card adding the usual seam allowance, as shown in fig. 60 and 62.

Fig. 59 *Small 'Fruit Basket' quilt (48" or 122 cm square)*

Fig. 60 *Tracing off the shapes from
the full scale drawing*

Also make some long templates to use for the long strips. To
save tracing the extra long strips, these templates can be used
and the measurement transferred from the drawing to the
fabric, as shown in fig. 63.

To make a long template

Draw on to card, two parallel lines exactly 2.5 cm [or 1 in]
apart, and about 46 cm [or 18 in] long. On both ends draw in
angles of 45°, as shown in fig. 61. The length of this template
is not specified, as it is to be used generally throughout the
fruit basket block. Add a 6 mm [or ¼ in] seam allowance on
all sides. Make two or three of these for general use. The 45°
angle is to be used on all the outer edges of the central
diamond fruit basket shape.

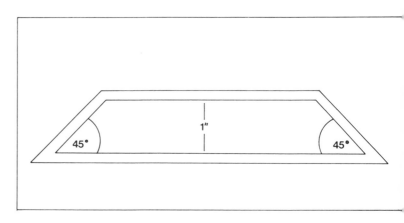

Fig. 61 *Making a long template*

Fig. 62 *Making the templates*

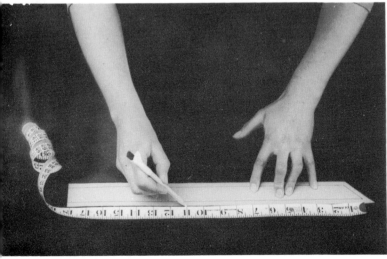

Fig. 63 *Using the long template*

Construction

Begin to piece the fruit basket at the top of the diamond block. Trace this first triangle from your drawing. Make the template and cut out this shape in fabric. Work steadily down the rows, making up six rows at a time. Then stop to join these rows together. The first six rows are straight forward, as they are plain. They can be cut out by using the long template, as shown in fig. 63. Draw around your template, stopping at the approximate length. Then measure the exact length from the drawing and transfer that measurement on to the fabric. When transferring this measurement, always make sure you measure from seam to seam line on your material, and then add an extra 6 mm [or ¼ in] seam allowance on each end.

Continue to construct the fruit basket in rows, until you come to the top of the basket handle. Then stop, and construct separate units B, C and D, as shown in fig. 64. These three units can be joined. Continue to work through the remainder of the block, on the strips contained in unit E, until the fruit basket image is complete.

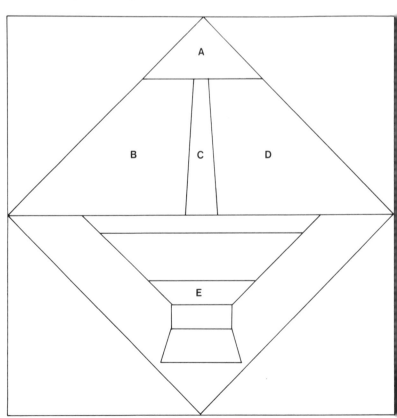

Fig. 64 *Constructing the 'Fruit Basket' quilt*

Next construct the surrounding black background area. The black area is made out of several pieces of fabric, as shown in fig. 65.

Cut eight of each of these shapes and sew them together in order, as shown in fig. 65. You will now have 8 large triangles. Pair these triangles up to form four larger triangles and sew these to the corners of the fruit basket diamond, as shown in fig. 59.

Prepare two fabric frames 4 cm [or 1½ in] wide, and sew one around the edges (as described in chapter 2). Keep the other frame aside for finishing off.

Quilting

Prepare the pieced wallhanging for quilting in the usual manner and machine or hand quilt. In the central block it is quite adequate to quilt on the lines running horizontally and the basket handle.

Finishing off

Finish off all the ends of cotton, use the prepared frame to complete the quilt, as described in chapter 2, under framing the quilt.

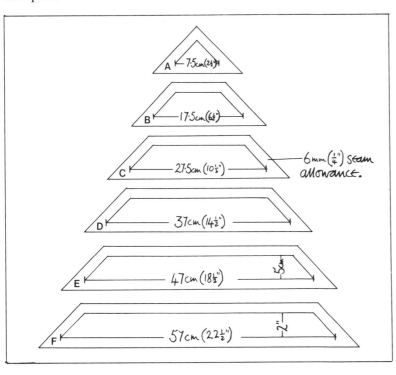

Fig. 65 *Pieces needed for the corner sections*

7. THE 'FLYING DUCKS' QUILT

This idea came from seeing a 'King Penguin' book on ducks. The dust wrapper was so spectacular, and seemed to lend itself ideally to a quilt design. I have used the traditional pattern, 'Streak of Lightning' or 'Zig-Zag', around the flying ducks, to represent water. Surrounding this is a border of various tones of green, forming a stylised design of rushes and reeds. The size of the finished quilt is 261 cm [or 103 in] × 213 cm [or 84 in].

Three patterns are needed for this quilt, the duck block, the 'streak of lightning', and the rushes.

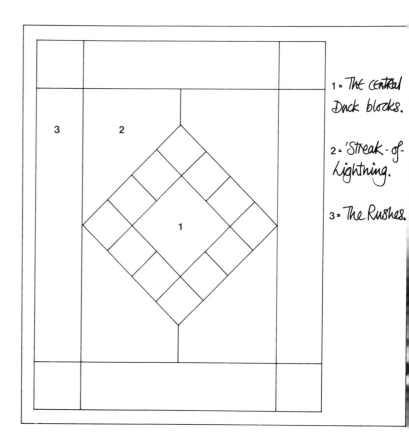

1 = The central Duck blocks.

2 = 'Streak-of-Lightning.

3 = The Rushes.

Fig. 66 *General construction of the different areas*

Materials needed

All fabrics used are 36 in wide.
Dark blue—1.75 m [or 2 yd]
Mid blue—2 m [or 2¼ yd]
Light blue—2 m [or 2¼ yd]
Black—2 m [or 2¼ yd]
Grey print—1 m [or 1 yd]
Blue print—1 m [or 1 yd]
Green print—1 m [or 1 yd]
Four shades of green—1.5 m [or 1¾ yd] of each.
Backing fabric—10 m [or 10½ yd]
Wadding (36 in wide)—10 m [or 10½ yd]

The duck block

The large central block measures 51 cm [or 20 in] square. The smaller ones measure 25.5 cm [or 10 in] square.

Draw the block out to the actual sizes, on graph paper, referring to fig. 67. Draw the smaller block first and then the larger one (for this just double the measurements).

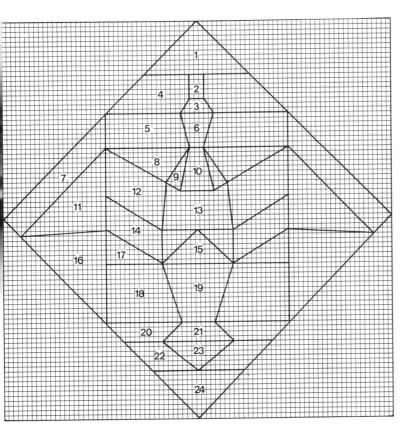

Fig. 67 *The 'Duck' block*

77

Trace the entire block on to tracing paper, and add the numbers shown in fig. 67. This is just for reference, you may need to refer to the size and shape of the templates later, when making the block. Add the numbers to the graph paper drawing as well, and cut these shapes out.

Several of the shapes are duplicated from one side of the duck to the other, so only cut out the necessary templates. Paste them down to card and on each one add the seam allowance of 6 mm [or ¼] on all sides. It is a good idea to mark the pieces that make up the background; it makes it clearer to sort the pieces when cutting out.

Cut out the necessary pieces to make six smaller duck blocks on a blue printed background, and six on a grey printed background. Then cut the pieces out for the large central duck block.

To construct the duck block
Lay all of the cut out shapes in position beside the tracing paper drawing, so that you can refer to the various numbered shapes.

Fig. 68 *Constructing the 'Duck'*
block I

Begin by studying the construction plan I (fig. 68), and piece these shapes together, one step at a time. Replace them in position on the table, until you have pieced all these sections together. Move on to construction plan II (fig. 69) and piece these sections together. Continue through the construction plan III (fig. 70). This leaves you with four sections to piece together.

Fig. 69 *Constructing the 'Duck' block II*

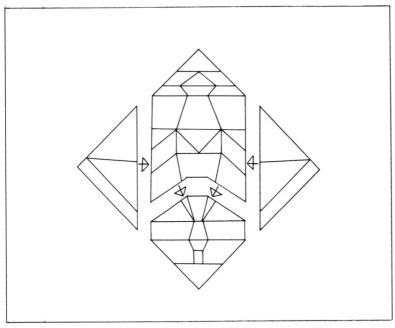

Fig. 70 *Constructing the 'Duck' block III*

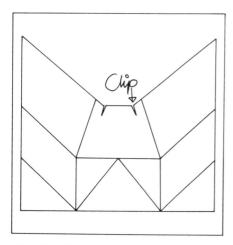

Fig. 71 *Clipping the angles seam*

The seam line joining the neck to the body of the duck is a little tricky. However, if you clip into the angled point this should make it possible to sew, producing an angled seam at this point (See fig. 71). When sewing the clipped piece, leave the needle down at the angled point, lift up the presser foot, and rearrange the fabric in the new direction of the seam.

When this is complete, it only remains to add the two triangular pieces, the tips of the wings, to the block.

'Streak of lightning' or 'zig-zag'

The basic construction of this design is very simple, and it requires only one template, a triangle. Draw the triangle shape on to graph paper, making the lower edge 10 cm [or 4 in] long and the central length 10 cm [or 4 in] long as shown in fig. 73. Paste this shape to card and add the usual 6 mm [or ¼ in] seam allowance around the three sides, and cut the template out.

Find the centre of the lower edge and mark this point with a small 'V'. This will allow you to mark this point with chalk when cutting out. It helps with the construction later on.

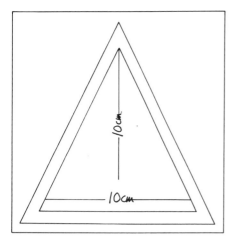

Fig. 73 *'Streak-of-lightning' template*

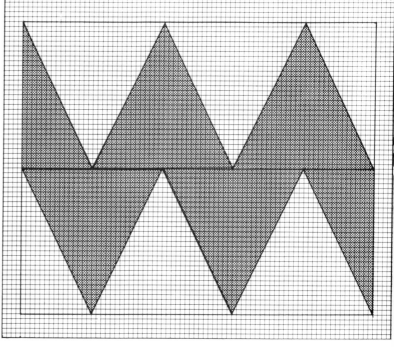

Fig. 72 *'Zig-Zag' or 'Streak-of-lightning'*

80

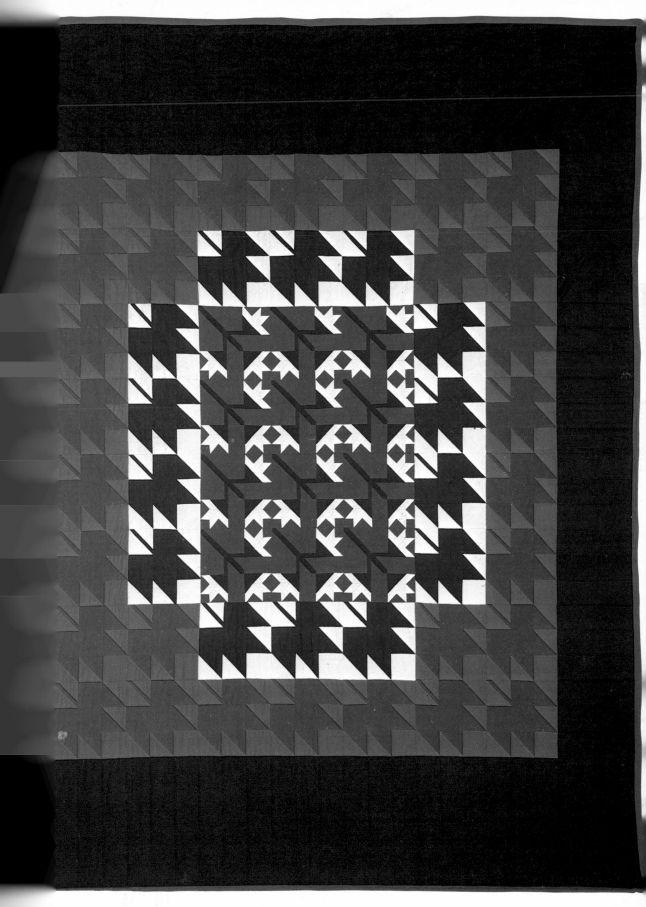

'utting out

'ou will need:

12—Dark blue triangles.
36—Mid blue triangles.
44—Light blue triangles.

'ivide these triangles into four separate piles:

3, dark blue.
4, mid blue.
6, light blue.

ew the triangles together in four separate quarters, working
 vertical construction rows. Sew the triangles in pairs, then
ress and join the pairs to form the rows (see fig. 74 and 75).
Vhen joining each row, make use of the mark in the central
osition on the lower edge of the triangle. Match this to the
oint of the triangle on the next row, as shown in fig. 75.

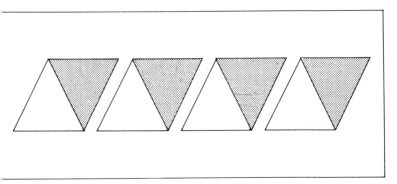

Fig. 74 'Streak-of-lightning'
section 2

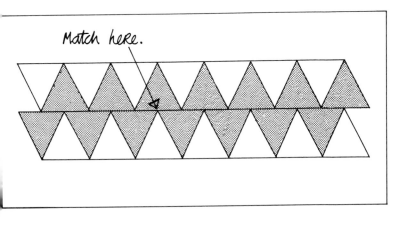

Fig. 75 Joining the pieces together

81

After piecing these four sections, sew them together in pairs as shown in fig. 76. Leave the last 6 mm [or ¼ in] of this seam open, to make it easier to set in the central diamond shape.

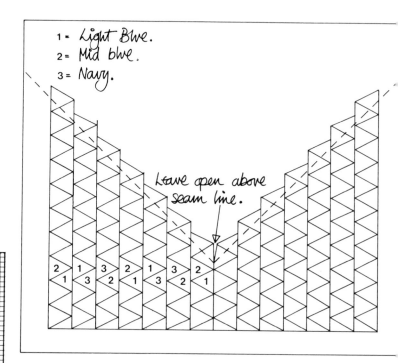

Fig. 76 *Matching the rows*

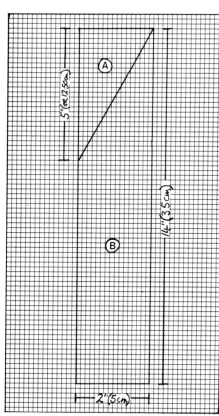

Fig. 77 *Making the 'rushes' templates A and B*

The rushes

Draw a rectangle on graph paper, measuring 35.5 cm [or 14 in] × 5 cm [or 2 in]. Measure 12.5 cm [or 5 in] down on one of the long sides, and join this point to the opposite top corner, to form the angle of the rush. Cut both shapes out (the rush and the background) and paste them on to card to form the two templates needed. Add the seam allowances around all edges.

Cutting out

Cut out 134 of the template 'A' all in black fabric. And 134 of the template 'E', equally divided between the four tones of green fabric.

Sew one template 'A' to each of the rushes (template B). Then sew two lots of 29 of the rushes together, side by side. This will form the top and lower edges. Use 76 rushes for the two remaining edges, on the sides, sewing them in four lots of 19 (see fig. 66).

82

onstruct the corner pieces by drawing a square on graph
aper, measuring 35.5 cm [or 14 in] on all sides. Divide this
to diagonal strips 5 cm [or 2 in] in width. Cut these out to
rm the templates, and make up four of these blocks, using
e same four tones of green fabric. (See fig. 79)

onstructing the quilt
he central duck blocks
onstruct section 'A', as shown in fig. 80, placing the large
lock in the centre of the twelve smaller duck blocks. Quilt
is unit separately.

Streak of lightning' and the rushes
iece units B and C together, as shown in fig. 80. Begin with
e 'streak of lightning' section, and add a row of 29 rushes to
e longer of the outside border edges. It may be necessary to
ke 2 cm [or ¾ in] off of each end to make it fit exactly.

oin the corner pieces (fig. 79) to the ends of the short rows
f 19 rushes. Sew to the sides of units B and C, as shown in
g. 80. Quilt both unit B and C separately.

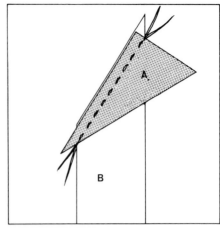

Fig. 78 *Sewing A to B*

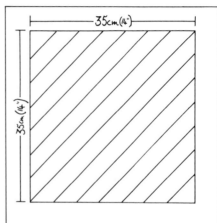

Fig. 79 *The corner sections for the
'Flying Ducks' quilt*

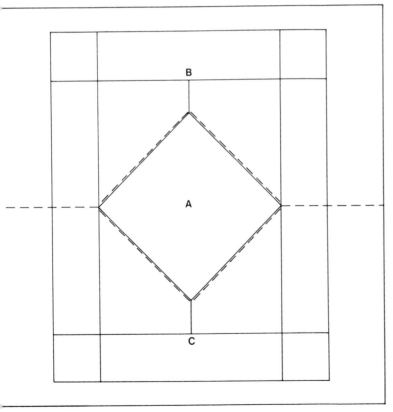

Fig. 80 *Constructing the whole
quilt*

83

Finishing the quilt

Sew these three units together, by joining units B and C and then setting in the central diamond. Take special care when approaching the points. Leave the sewing needle down when you reach the actual points, lift the presser foot and rearrang the fabric to steer into the angle of the next seam. (Refer to chapter 2, 'framing the quilt' for more details of this method

Finish the back of the quilt by pressing and taping (as described in chapter 2). Then bind the edges to complete the quilt.

Fig. 81 Six examples of the Kaleidoscope view

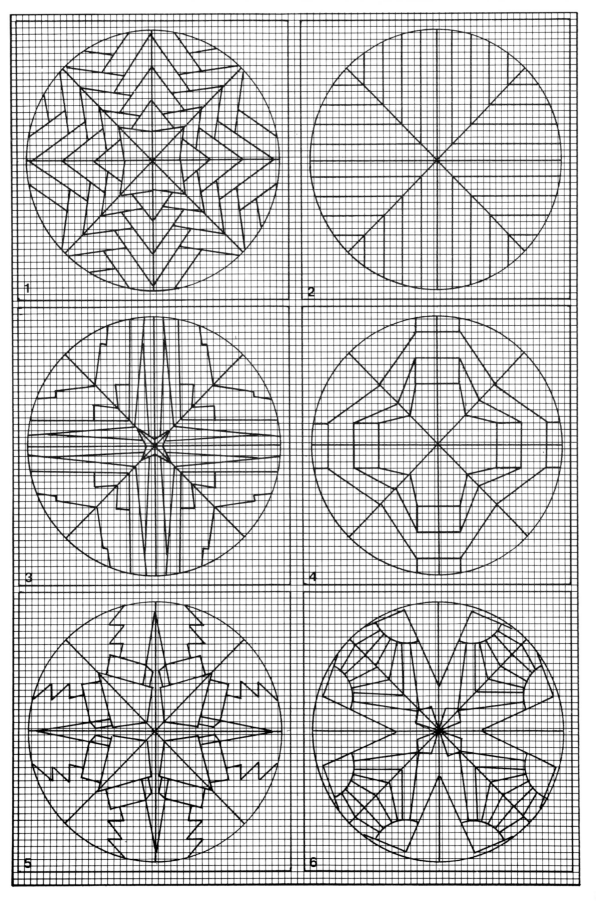

85

8. KALEIDOSCOPE QUILTS

Kaleidoscopes are a great source of inspiration for quilt designs. After looking through one or two, I discovered the best type of kaleidoscope for this use seems to be the kind that is completely transparent and clear, without any beads or coloured shapes, simply eight clear images reflecting from the mirrors. I found these images very exciting, and proceeded to fix the kaleidoscope into position, leaving both hands free to draw things that I saw through it. As a result I came up again with endless possibilities. A few are shown in fig. 81.

Design '1' seemed to be very strong, so I thought it best to continue the lines out at the corners and make it into a regular square block design. The result is shown in fig. 82.

Fig. 82 *The 'Kaleidoscope I' block*

The easiest way to break down any of these kaleidoscope designs, is into eight sections, radiating from the centre. One of these sections for design '1' is shown in fig. 83.

The size of the finished block is 25.5 cm [or 10 in]. Therefore the length of the top edge of the section in fig. 83 is 12.75 [or 5 in]. Draw this section up on graph paper. Cut each piece out and mark the grain line. Also number the pieces as shown in fig. 83. Paste these pieces down on to card and make the templates.

Cutting out
Cut four of the sections, as shown in fig. 83, using the templates the correct way up. Cut another four sections, using the template up-side-down. This will form the sectional pairs needed for the whole block, as shown in fig. 84.

Piecing the block
Refer back to fig. 83 and begin piecing at the outside edge. Piece number 9 and 10 together. Press the seam open, then add number 8, then number 7, and so on, until you reach the centre point with number 1.

Make up all eight sections in this manner. Then pair them together to form four squares. Match the seams by pinning and tacking, if necessary. Sew the four squares together to form the final block.

Making the kaleidoscope quilt
The finished size of the quilt is 99 cm [or 39 in] square.

Material needed:
All fabric is 36 in wide.
Black—80 cm [or 1 yd]
Cream—50 cm [or ½ yd]
Light green—50 cm [or ½ yd]
Mid green—50 cm [or ½ yd]
Dark green—1.5 m [or 1¾ yd]
Light blue—1.5 m [or 1¾ yd]
Mid blue—1.5 m [or 1¾ yd]
Dark blue—1.5 m [or 1¾ yd]
Backing fabric—2.5 m [or 2½ yd]
Wadding (36 in wide)—2.5 m [or 2½ yd]

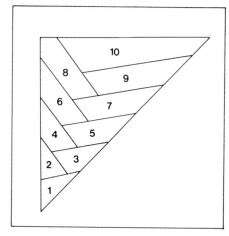

Fig. 83 *One section of the 'Kaleidoscope' block*

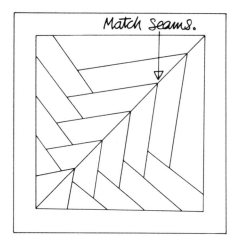

Fig. 84 *Two sections paired together for the 'Kaleidoscope' block*

Make up nine kaleidoscope blocks as described above. Sew them together in three rows of three blocks each, and join ti rows together.

Make paper patterns for the border frames. Four full frame: are needed, plus the four corner insets, which all measure 2. cm [or 1 in] wide. (Refer to the photograph of this quilt.) Ci these shapes out in the appropriate fabric.

Sew each side together first, as shown in fig. 85. Inset the corner bands and sew this wide frame around the central block section. The sewing method for this is described in chapter 2 (under 'framing the quilt').

Quilting and finishing off
Prepare the whole quilt by pinning the layers together etc. a quilt in the usual manner.

Finish off, by adding another frame and hand sewing it on t back. Insert a channel of fabric to hold a wooden rod, by which to hang the quilt (as described in chapter 2).

An alternative design
An alternative way of using this design is to work in exactly the same way until you have pieced the four squares togethe Then instead of setting them on a central axis, place these squares side by side, as shown in layout drawing 'K' on page 4

The two layout drawings J and K, on pages 44 and 45, are t help you experiment with the use of colour. Lay a sheet of tracing paper over them and try out different combinations o colour, using crayons.

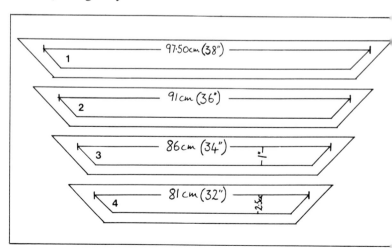

Fig. 85 *The four pieces that form the frame for the 'Kaleidoscope' quilt*

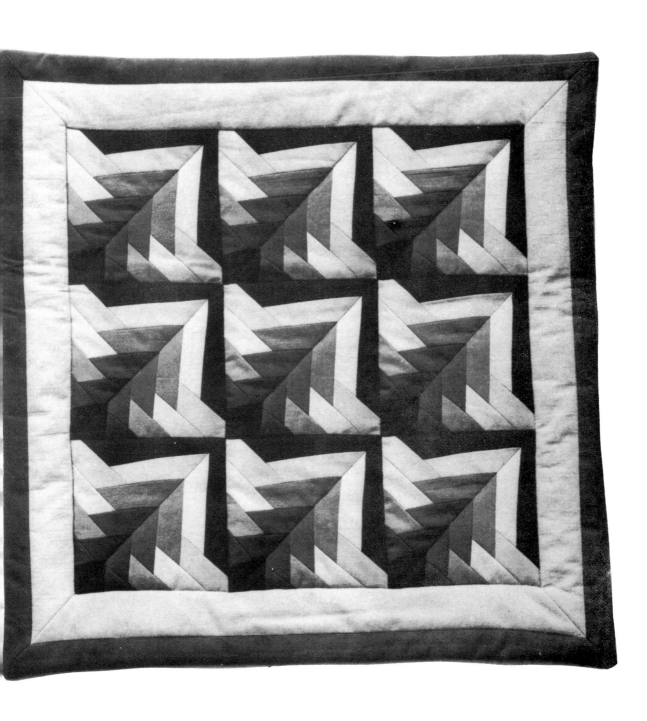

Kaleidoscope Variation

9. EGYPTIAN WALLHANGING

The design theme for this quilt came from a friend who commissioned a quilt from me. He asked for a quilt based on Egyptian art. I was delighted with the theme.

I spent a long time making preparatory drawings in the Egyptian section of the British Museum. I found the general colour combinations and forms very stunning and inspiring. Many of my studies were taken from their superb collection of Egyptian Mummies.

I produced several designs and he chose the Egyptian Quilt I (Scarab). After completing this quilt I went on to make one or two of the other designs I had drawn up.

The one described here is a wallhanging, measuring 104 cm [or 41 in] × 117 cm [or 46 in]. The central panel contains four sitting men. This seated figure is a stylized version of a figure that often appears in Egyptian hieroglyphics. At the top and bottom, there are lotus flowers, the stems of which continue down each side.

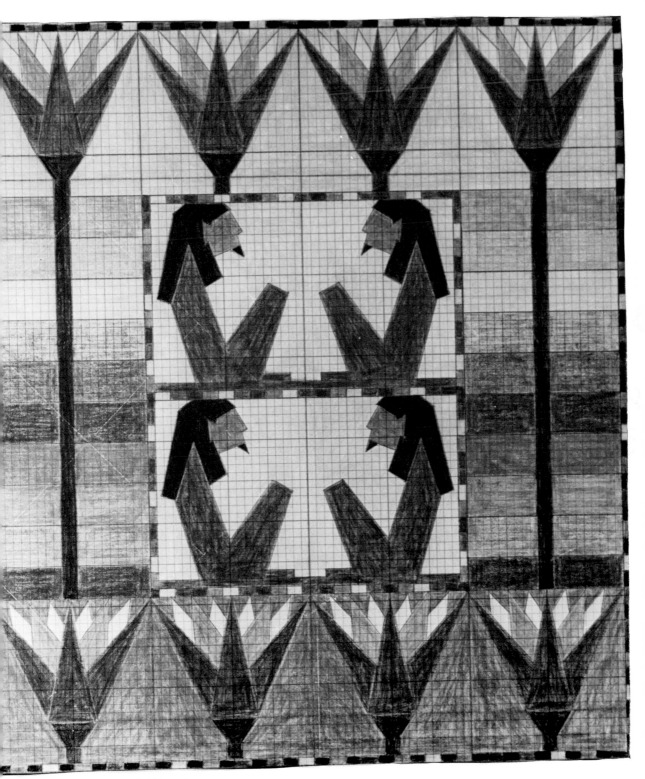

Design for Egyptian Wallhanging

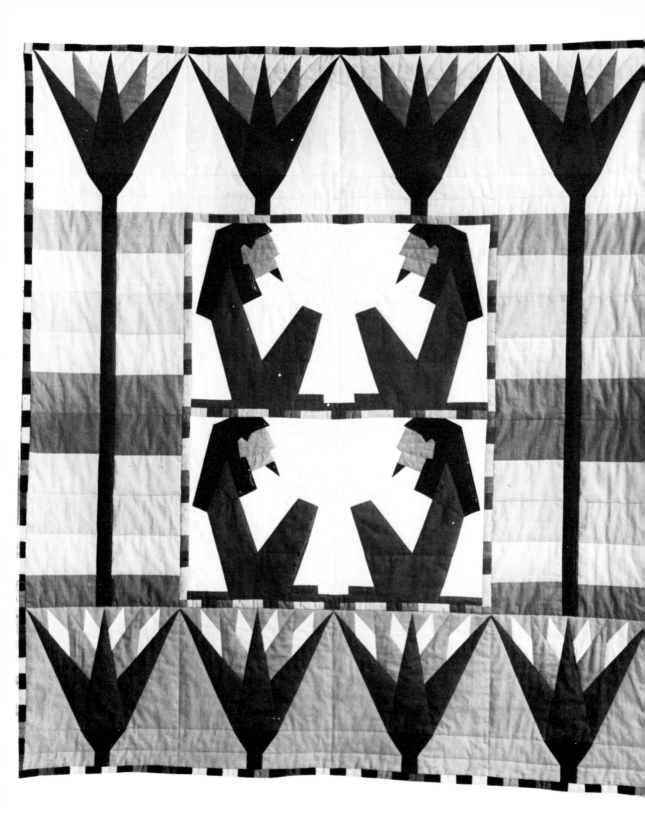

Materials needed:

All fabrics are 36 in wide.

Light blue—25 cm [or ¼ yd]
Mid blue—25 cm [or ¼ yd]
Slate blue—1.5 m [or 1¾ yd]
Cream—75 cm [or ¾ yd]
Black—75 cm [or ¾ yd]
Rust—75 cm [or ¾ yd]
Light grey—75 cm [or ¾ yd)
Dark grey—10 cm [or ⅛ yd]
Light green—25 cm [or ¼ yd]
Beige—10 cm [or ⅛ yd]
Olive—10 cm [or ⅛ yd]
Brown—25 cm [or ¼ yd]
Camel—10 cm [or ⅛ yd]
Dark beige—25 cm [or ¼ yd]
Light olive—10 cm [or ⅛ yd]
Dark brown—10 cm [or ⅛ yd]
Backing fabric—2.3 m [or 2½ yd]
Wadding (36 in wide)—2.3 m [or 2½ yd]

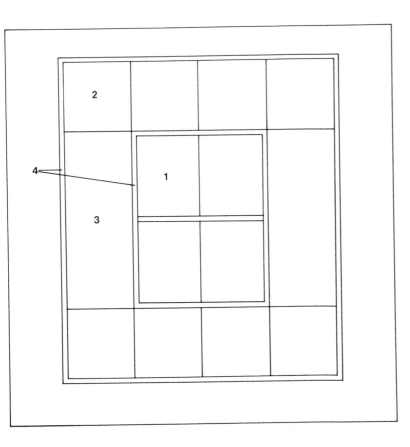

Fig. 86 *Basic construction of the 'Egyptian' Wallhanging*

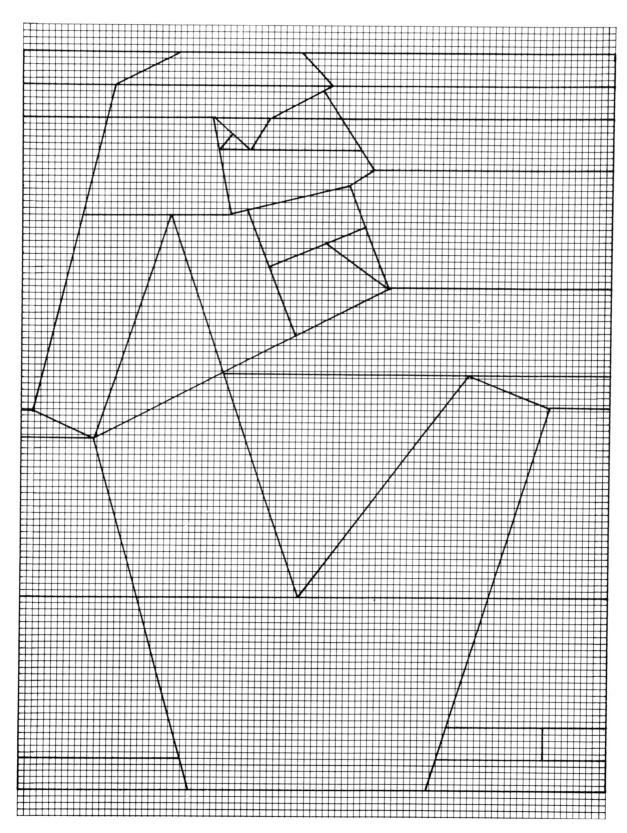

Fig. 87 *The 'Egyptian Man' block*

General construction of the quilt
This quilt is made up of the four units shown in fig. 86.

1 The Egyptian man block.
2 The Lotus flower block.
3 Landscape colour block.
4 The framings.

The Egyptian man block

Draw up the finished block on graph paper, making the size of the block 24 cm [or $9\frac{1}{2}$ in] $\times$ 29 cm [or $11\frac{1}{2}$ in]. Take the general proportions within the block from the drawing (fig. 87).

Copy the whole drawing on to tracing paper and number both drawings with the numbers indicated in fig. 88a.

Proceed in the usual manner, and make the necessary templates.

Cut out the required number of pieces for this block in the appropriate colours; the body in State Blue, his hair and beard in black, face in rust and background in cream.

Constructing the block

To make construction easier, divide the block into units, as shown in fig. 88b.

Unit 'A'
This is straight forward. Piece templates 1, 2 and 3 together to form the top strip, then 4, 5, 6 and 7, to form the second strip, and piece them together.

Unit 'B'
Begin by piecing this unit with numbers 10 and 37. Then sew this to 11 and 12, adding 13 and finally 36 and 9.

Unit 'C'
Begin with numbers 20 and 19, then 15, adding 14, 16, 17 and 18.

Unit 'D' and 'E'
These are separate templates, and only added later when units 'B' and 'C' have been joined.

95

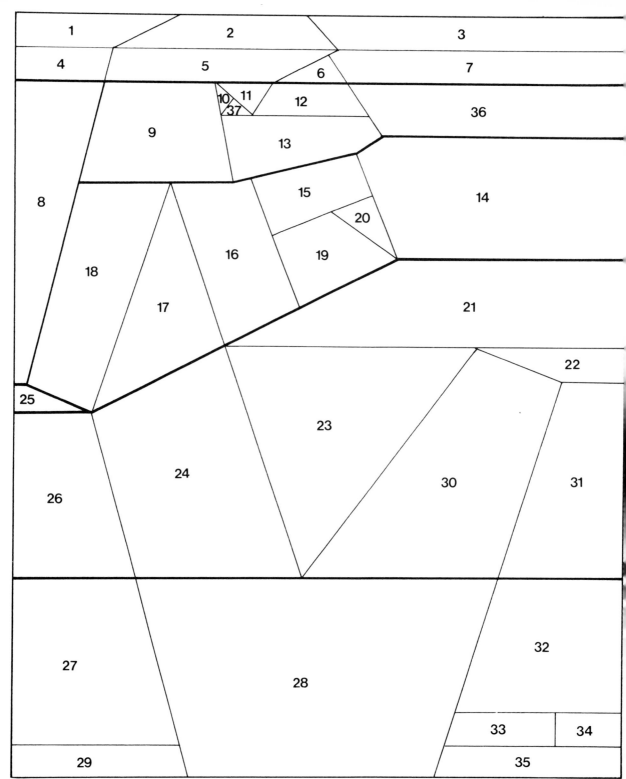

Fig. 88a *The numbered templates*

Unit 'F'

Sew 26, 24, 23 and 30 together. Add number 31, leaving the last 6 mm [or ¼ in] of the seam unsewn on the side nearest number 22. Sew on piece number 22, matching the seams carefully and forming the angle needed at the point between 30 and 31 (see chapter 2, 'framing the quilt', for detailed description.)

Unit 'G'

Form unit G by sewing 27 to 29, then 33 to 34, adding 32 and 35. Sew these two units to number 28.

Having pieced all these units separately, sew the units together. First A, B and C, next adding F and G. Again there are some angled seams to cope with, so match the seams carefully and refer to chapter 2 for more details.

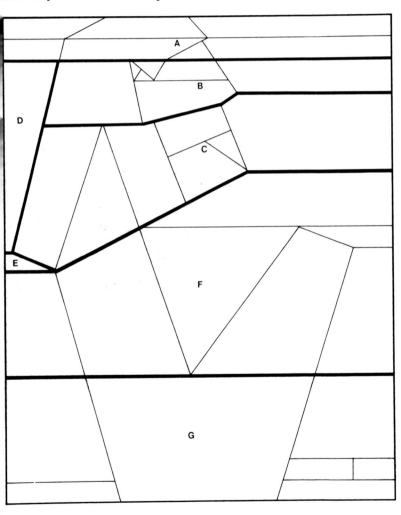

Fig. 88b *The construction units*

Cut out and make the four blocks of the Egyptian man, making them in pairs.

The lotus flower block

Draw the lotus flower block on to graph paper making the finished size of the block 25.5 cm [or 10 in] square. Refer to fig. 89. Make a tracing of this drawing, and number both drawings as in fig. 89. Cut out the pieces from the graph paper drawing, and make the templates by pasting these shapes to card, and adding the usual seam allowance of 6 mm [or ¼ in] around each shape.

Begin to piece this block by sewing 10 and 12 together, then 9 and 14. Next add numbers 11 and 13. Then sew these two units to number 8. Sew numbers 5 and 6 to this, adding the central number 7. Finally add the last two strips that are made up of 3 and 4, and 1 and 2 (See fig. 90).

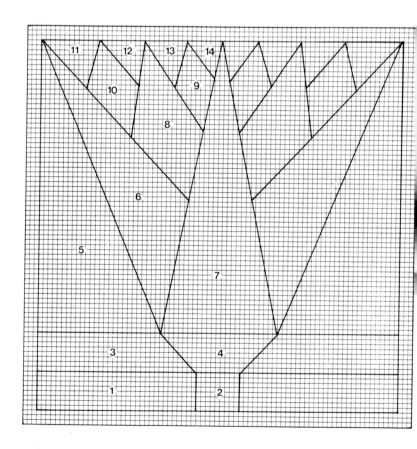

Fig. 89 *The 'Lotus Flower' block*

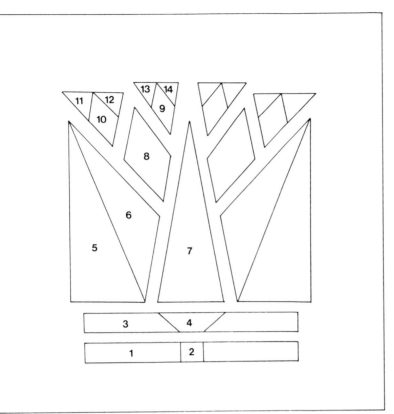

Fig. 90 *Constructing the 'Lotus Flower' block*

Fig. 91 *Landscape colour block— Unit 3*

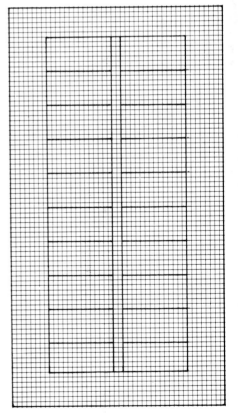

Landscape colour blocks (unit 3)

These two blocks are very straight forward, and only three templates are needed.

The central stem measures 2.5 cm [or 1 in] wide × 62 cm [or 24½ in]. Make one template this size, and add the 6 mm [or ¼ in] seam allowances around all edges. Cut out two pieces of slate blue coloured fabric from this pattern.

The rectangles forming the landscape behind the stem are all 6.3 cm [or 2½ in] × 11.4 cm [or 2½ in]. The last rectangle at the base of the lotus stem measures 5 cm [or 2 in] × 11.4 cm [or 4½ in]. Again these measurements are all from seam to seam, therefore seam allowances must be added to make the templates.

Cut out the necessary pieces of fabric and sew them together in the correct order, referring to fig. 91. Beginning from the top, cut out 4 templates of each of the following colours; dark grey, light grey, light green, light olive, olive, brown, camel, biege, light olive and brown. Sew them together in this order.

The framings

This quilt has a border frame, and also one surrounding the central 'Egyptian man' blocks. In both cases, these are made up of pieces measuring 1.25 cm [or ½ in] × 2.5 cm [or 1 in], plus 6 mm [or ¼ in] seam allowances for the templates.

The central frame uses brown, slate blue, camel and light green, in rotation. The outer frame uses black alternating with each of the colours used in the central frame.

To construct the total quilt

Sew the two pairs of the 'Egyptian man' blocks together, and add the inner frames.

Make up four lotus flower blocks with the light grey background, and four with the rust coloured background, using the three tones of blue for the flower in both blocks. Join these together in two rows, each of four lotus flowers. Join one landscape colour block (unit three) to each side of the central block. Join one row of lotus flowers to the top of the central block and one row to the bottom. Finally, add the outer frame.

Quilting and finishing

Cut the backing fabric, two lengths 112 cm [or 44 in] long, and join. Cut off the surplus fabric.

Lay the wadding over this, then the pieced work. Prepare and quilt in the usual way and finish off by binding the edges.

10. DYEING THE FABRIC

Many quiltmakers I have spoken to have endless searches to find the particular colour fabric that they require for a design. I, too, went through endless torment in this pursuit. There seemed only one possible solution, and this was to dye my own fabric!

I was lucky enough to find a place available for a weekend course in chemical dyeing with Roy Russell and Wilma Hollist, of Muswell Hill Weavers, 65, Rosebery Road, London N10 2LE. They sell dyes in small quantities and general equipment for dyeing. It was an extremely exciting weekend for me. We were shown how to use four different types of dye, including one which was ideal to use with cotton fibre. This dye is 'cold water dye' or 'fibre reactive dye', (in the trade it is sometimes known as 'Procion M. dye'). It is often used in tie dyeing, or batik. The information that was given throughout the weekend was invaluable.

Cold water, or fibre reactive dye is ideal for dyeing cotton fabric, and proves to be very fast both when washed and when exposed to the light. The technique of dyeing, described below, can easily be done in your kitchen.

Fig. 92 *Equipment needed for dyeing*

1. *Kitchen scales*
2. *Plastic bowls*
3. *Fabric samples*
4. *Glass rods*
5. *Syringes*
6. *Small scales for weighing dye powder*
7. *Measuring jug*
8. *Soda solution*
9. *Dye*
10. *Beakers*
11. *Salt solution*
12. *Bottle and funnel*

101

Equipment needed

The only large pieces of equipment needed are your cooker, and a washing machine.

The cooker

Any type of cooker will do, or just a hot plate to heat a cauldron of water.

The washing machine

This is used to dye large lengths of fabric. It must be the type that can be turned on or off when you wish (An automatic type would not be suitable). It is ideally suited to keep the fabric moving with the agitator. There is plenty of room in the average sized tub to dye about 4 m of fabric. There must be enough room to allow the fabric to float around freely in the water, without creasing up. If there is not enough room and you try to dye too much fabric in this amount of water, you will undoubtedly have an uneven dye as a result.

Plastic beakers

These are used to mix the dye in and also for measuring dye solution.

Plastic basins

Used to dye up fabric samples.

Syringes

These are used to measure dye solution in small quantities.

Glass rods

Are used to stir the fabric samples and dye solution.

Scales and weights

These are used to weigh the dye powder accurately.

A saucepan

Used to boil up fabric samples.

Large cauldron

This is used to boil up a length of fabric.

Large wooden spoon

For stirring the solution on a large scale.

Rubber gloves
For protection against the dye solution.

Mask and overalls
For protection against dye.

Cider bottles
To mix dye solution in.

Funnel
For adding liquid to bottles.

The measures used in the dyeing methods given below are:
For liquid measure—
(ml) millilitres (1000 ml = 1 l)
(l) litres (1 litre = about 1¾ pt)
For solid measure—
(gm) grams (1000 gm = 1 kilogram)
(kg) kilogram (1 kg = 2 lb 3¼ oz)

When using both solid and liquid measures, 1 gm is approximately equal to 1 ml.

Materials needed:
  Dye.
  Salt.
  Soda (washing soda).
  Cotton fabric.
  Washing powder.

I always dye a small sample of fabric first of all. I measure and record the amounts of fabric, water, dye solution and soda solution involved. When I am satisfied with the colour produced I go ahead and dye up a length of fabric on a large scale, multiplying the dye, water, and salt and soda solutions accordingly.

Dyeing a sample
Cut out a rectangular piece of cotton fabric, measuring 10 cm × 20 cm [or 4 in × 8 in]. This will weigh approximately 3.5 gm using a medium weight cotton fabric.

To dye a very fine or heavier weight cotton find out how much it weighs per metre, and calculate the size of the rectangular piece needed to weigh the same 3.5 gm.

Gauge the correct weight of the fabric before you begin to dye; the amounts of dye solution, salt, soda and water needed in the process are always related to the fabric weight.

1 Boil up the sample piece of fabric for five minutes in water and a little detergent. This is to remove any dressing which may be in the fabric. Rinse thoroughly and leave the fabric soaking in cold water.

2 Make a small amount of dye solution. Weigh 1 gm of dye powder and mix with a little cold water, using a glass rod. Make this into a paste consistency, and make sure there are no lumps in it.

Slowly add some hot water (not boiling) to this solution, until you reach the 100 ml mark on the beaker. You have now made a 1% solution of dye mixture—1 gm of dye powder to 100 ml of water. This seems the most convenient way of mixing the solution, as it has to be used in liquid form.

Mix the colours that you wish to use.

The dye solution cannot be stored in this liquid form as it will weaken in strength after three or four days. So fresh solution must be made each time you dye.

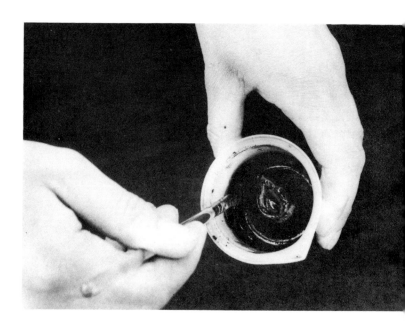

Fig. 93 *'Pasting-up' the dye*

104

3 Place enough cold water, in a bowl, to cover the sample easily, about 200 ml.

4 Add the measured amount of dye solution to this water. To produce a dark colour, use perhaps 100 ml of dye solution, for a pale wash use as little as 0.50 ml. Experiment with the amounts to give an idea of the tones you can achieve.

5 Stir the solution and place the soaked fabric into the dye bath. Make sure the fabric is completely covered and try to keep it fairly flat and not creased up, as this may produce uneven dyeing results. Allow the sample to soak in this solution for about 5 minutes, stirring occasionally (See fig. 94).

6 Remove the fabric sample from the dye bath. Then add 7 ml of the salt solution.

The salt solution is made by dissolving 250 gm salt into 1 l of boiling water. This can be stored in a large bottle and kept for use at any time.

7 Stir the solution, and replace the fabric sample. At this stage it is very important to keep the fabric moving in the solution. The salt solution makes the dye penetrate in the fabric. Leave the fabric in this solution for about 15 minutes, stirring frequently.

Fig. 94 *Immersing the fabric in the dye bath*

8 Remove the fabric from the dye bath and add 3.5 ml of soda solution.

This solution is made by dissolving 200 gm of washing soda in 1 l of hot water, and stirring until the crystals have disappeared. Again this solution can be kept in a bottle and used at any time.

Return the fabric sample again to the dye bath, keeping it fairly flat, and stir occasionally. Leave it in this solution for between 1 hour and 4 hours. The total penetration of the dye will have absolutely finished after 4 hours.

9 Remove the sample from the dye bath. Rinse it in cold water, before boiling it in clean water and a little detergent. This removes any of the 'loose' dye that is sitting in the fabric, thus leaving only the fast dyed fabric. Boil for 5 to 10 minutes.

10 Remove the fabric from the boiling water, and rinse very thoroughly, until the water is completely clear.

11 Allow the fabric sample to dry fully. Then assess the colour. It is often difficult to determine the final colour. It is only when the whole process has been completed and the fabric is dry that the true colour can be seen. Compare the sample with the colour you were hoping to achieve, then re-assess the dye amounts, and change them according to your needs. Perhaps you would like a darker tone, or lighter.

12 Always make a record of the amounts of dye you have used and pin this to the fabric sample. By doing this you will begin to build up a library of colour formulas, for reference.

Mixing colours
Basically the only colours that you need to begin are the three primary colours, red, blue and yellow. By mixing these in varying quantities you will be able to achieve a very large colour range. However, other intermediate colours are also available, which you may well find help to expand your colour range a little.

Colour matching

The freedom of colour choice obtained once you begin to dye your own fabrics is marvelous. It is possible to match almost any colour you wish. However, there are a few exceptions with this type of cold water dye. It is very difficult to obtain very dark colours or extremely bright colours. The whole range and quality of these dyes tend to be a more subdued.

To match a particular colour, work on the scale of the fabric sample as described above. You may have to repeat this whole process of dyeing the sample several times before achieving the colour you want.

As an example, assume you wish to match a sea green colour. To begin, guess the amounts of dye solution to use, say 20 ml of blue, and 30 ml of yellow. Go through the whole process of dyeing a sample piece of fabric using the method described above. When the sample is completely dry, compare it with the colour you are trying to match. Then re-assess the amounts of dye solution used. Perhaps you will need to add some more blue, or more of each colour. Decide how to achieve a nearer colour match, then change the formula of the dye solution, and go through the whole process again. At the end of this you will have two different coloured samples. Continue in this manner, until you achieve your goal, and match the colour required.

Of course the more samples you dye, the easier it becomes, because there is often a fabric sample that is fairly near the colour that you require.

Dyeing up a length of four metres

Find the exact colour you require by dyeing samples. Once you are satisfied with it, multiply all the measurements, the fabric weight, the dye solution, the salt and soda and water in proportion.

Fabric

Begin by preparing the fabric. The average washing machine can dye 4 m of cloth with ease. So cut off this length of fabric. Boil it up in a large cauldron, with a little detergent, to remove the dressing. Work out how many times larger this piece of fabric is compared to the fabric sample. In this case it is 180 times larger. Once this has been established multiply the other ingredients by the same amount, to achieve the same colour on the large piece of cloth as on the sample.

Water
You will need enough water to cover the cloth easily, allowing room to add the dye solution.

Dye solution
Multiply the amount of dye solution used on the sample by 180 and 'paste-up' this large amount of dye. It is a good idea to use cider bottles for this purpose. Paste up the dye in the same way as described in the sample method, but this time fill the bottles instead of the beakers. Shake the bottle well to make sure the solution is thoroughly mixed.

Salt
For this amount of fabric you will need to use 310 gm [or 10 oz] of salt. Make it into a solution by adding about $1\frac{1}{2}$ litres of boiling water and stir until the salt has dissolved.

Soda
For the 4 metres of fabric you will need to use about 112 gm [or 4 oz] of washing soda. Dissolve it in about $\frac{3}{4}$ litre of hot water. Stir until the crystals have disappeared.

The process for the dyeing is exactly the same as for the sample piece. Perhaps the time when the fabric is in the dye bath, with the salt solution, may be prolonged to about half an hour instead of quarter of an hour. In this period (as described earlier) it is very important to keep the fabric moving. The washing machine is ideal for this, so keep turning it on every 5–10 minutes. After it has been agitated, put on your rubber gloves and make sure the fabric isn't twisted up in knots. If it is unwind it so that the dye can penetrate evenly throughout the length of fabric.

Continue the dyeing process exactly as the sample. Finish by boiling up the fabric in detergent, either in the washing machine or in a large cauldron. Rinse thoroughly, as before.

General hints
Allow the fabric to dry and iron the creases out. Do not fold the fabric until it is completely aired and dry, as fading may occur on the fold lines if you fold it when damp. Store it in subdued light.

When choosing the fabric to dye, make sure it is made of 100% cotton, so that the dye will take to the fabric. Also

ake sure there is no permanent type of dressing. e.g. resin
ating. The dye will not penetrate through this. The best idea
to choose your fabric and buy a small quantity of it. Then
oceed to dye up a few samples to make sure the quality is
ght.

make sure that you obtain an even dye:
Always remove the fabric before adding any of the
solutions.
Have plenty of room for the fabric to move freely.
Keep stirring and moving the fabric.
Make sure the fabric is not bunched up or twisted.
Make sure you 'paste up' the dye solution thoroughly and
that it is totally dissolved, and without lumps.

11. APPENDIX

Cleaning quilts
Old quilts
If your quilt is very old and precious, it is advisable to get some expert help on how to clean it, possibly from the textil department in your local museum. However, if it is in good condition and the fabric is not frail or rotting, it would be al right to wash it, using the methods described below. If you are in doubt, always seek advise.

New quilts
When making contemporary quilts, we have the option whether to make it so that it can be washed or dry cleaned. Generally, when choosing the materials, we know how they should be cleaned. However, even with washable fabrics, it is always advisable to wash or boil them before use, as they ma not be colour fast or pre-shrunk.

Testing for colour fastness
If you are not sure whether all the fabrics used in your quilt are colour fast test them, by rubbing the fabric with a moistened piece of cotton wool. If no colour comes off on to the cotton wool, it is fast. If some of the colour has been taken off on to the cotton wool it would be advisable to dry clean the quilt. Do not attempt to test silks or velvets, they should be dry cleaned.

Hand washable quilts
These quilts must have fast, washable fabrics. The type of wadding to be used is usually a synthetic, polyester or courtelle wadding. These are completely washable. However, providing that your quilting is forming a close enough grid over the whole quilt, cotton wadding can also be used and washed perfectly successfully, although the shops will advise you to dry clean this type of wadding. If it is not adequately quilted, lumps may begin to form inside the quilt, after severa washes.

Washing

Wash your quilt in the bath. Run enough warm water to cover the quilt and add a small quantity of washing powder. Make sure it is fully dissolved before immersing the quilt. Gently agitate the quilt without lifting it from the water. Avoid rubbing. Agitate for several minutes then pull out the plug, letting the water drain away. Gently squeeze the surplus water out. Replace the plug and run warm rinsing water into the bath. Agitate again and then let the water out, squeezing the surplus water out as before. Repeat the rinses at least three or four times or until no sign of detergent is left.

Drying

Find someone to help you remove the quilt from the bath, as it will be very heavy. At this point give the quilt a short spin if it will fit easily into the tub. If not squeeze the excess water out by rolling the quilt in several towels.

Choose a fine day and hang the quilt over a padded washing line. You can pad it by wrapping some white towels or sheeting around the line. This is to prevent marks appearing across the centre of the quilt. Alternatively, lay the quilt flat on a lawn with a sheet underneath it. In both cases avoid direct sunlight. A light, airy summer's day is ideal.

Creases or wrinkles can be removed by running a steam iron just over the top surface of the quilt, barely touching it. Do not press hard.

Dry cleaning a quilt

This is necessary if you find that the colours are not fast on your quilt, or if it is made of unwashable fabrics such as velvets or silks and satins. Perhaps the quilt is just too heavy and bulky to be washed, or the fabric used has not been pre-shrunk. Choose a specialist cleaner, one that is recommended in your area.

Useful Addresses

Strawberry Fayre,
Stockbridge
Hampshire.
Jenny and Alec Hutchison.

A good range of patchwork quilts are on view and for sale, both old and new. Books on the subject. A good range of fabrics, batting (or wadding), quilting threads, also quilting hoops are available, most of these items are imported from America.

Twenty One Antiques,
21 Chalk Farm Road,
London, NW1.
Joen and Tony Lask.

An excellent collection of quilts are for sale here. They also supply quilting equipment and books.

Liberty and Co. Ltd.,
Regent Street,
London, W1R 6AH.

An excellent range of Liberty designs, printed on fine cotton fabric.

John Lewis,
Oxford Street,
London, NW1.

A large selection of dress fabric are available.

Laura Ashley,
71, Lower Sloane St.,
London, SW1.

Various printed cotton fabrics. They also sell scrap bags, containing off cuts of material.

Wolfin and Son Ltd.
64, Great Tichfield St.,
London, W1.

Suppliers of plain cloths. Cotton calico, bleached and unbleached in various weights. Wadding by the metre or piece.

Muswell Hill Weavers,
65, Rosebery Road,
London, N10 2LE.
Roy Russell and Wilma Hollist

Dyes for sale by mail order, in small quantities. Also, dyeing equipment, beakers, glass rods, syringes etc.

Uni-DYE,
PO Box No 10.
Ilkley,
West Yorkshire.
LS29 9HY.

Dyestuffs and fixatives in small quantities.

The White Fleece,
17, Glendower Place,
London, SW7.

Specialist, dry cleaners.

Places to Visit

Abbot Hall, Museum of Lakeland Life, Kendal, Cumbria.	Room settings, including some quilts.
The American Museum, Claverton Manor, Bath, BA2 7BD.	A good collection of American patchwork quilts permanently on display, throughout the summer months.
Beamish Open Air Museum, Beamish, County Durham.	A large collection of quilts.
Castle Howard Costume Galleries, The Stables, Castle Howard, York.	One or two quilts in their collection.
Shipley Art Gallery Prince Consort Road, Gateshead, NE8 4JB.	A good information service available on quilts and quilting.
Ulster Folk and Transport Museum, Cultra Manor, Holywood, Co. Down, Northern Ireland.	A very large collection of quilts from Ireland.
Welsh Folk Museum, St Fagans, Cardiff.	They have a collection of quilts (Phone for an appointment to view.)
Victoria and Albert Museum, South Kensington, London, SW7 2RL.	A few quilts are on display. Appointments can be made to see other quilts in their collection

Recommended book list

AUTHOR	TITLE	PUBLISHER
Sheila Betterton	'Quilts and coverlets from the American Museum in Britain.'	The American Museum in Britain
Jinny Beyer	'Patchwork Patterns'	E.P.M. Publications McLean, Virginia
Robert Bishop	'New Discoveries in American Quilts'	E.P. Dutton & Company Inc., New York
Robert Bishop, and Elizabeth Safanda	'A Gallery of Amish Quilts'	E.P. Dutton & Company Inc., New York
Ruth E. Finley	'Old Patchwork Quilts and the Women who Made Them'	Grosset and Dunlap, New York
Mavis Fitzrandolph	'Traditional Quilting'	Batsford, London
Beth Gutcheon	'The Perfect Patchwork Primer'	Penguin Books
Beth and Jeffrey Gutcheon	'The Quilt Design Book'	Rawson Associates Publishers, Inc., New York
Phyllis Haders	'Sunshine and Shadow. The Amish and Their Quilts'	Universe Books, New York
Carrie A. Hall and Rose G. Kretsinger	'The Romance of the Patchwork Quilt in America'	Bonanza Books, New York
Jonathan Holstein	'The Pieced Quilt. An American design Tradition'	Galahad Books New York
Carter Houck and Myron Miller	'American Quilts and how to make them'	Pelham Books, London
Marguerite Ickis	'The Standard Book of Quiltmaking and Collecting'	Dover Publications Inc., New York
Michael James	'The Quiltmakers Handbook'	A Spectrum Book, Prentice-Hall Inc., New Jersey
Ruby McKim	'101 Patchwork Patterns'	Dover Publications Inc., New York
Patsy and Myron Orlofsky	'Quilts in America'	McGraw Hill Book Company

BIBLIOGRAPHY

'The Perfect Patchwork Primer'—Beth Gutcheon.

'101 Patchwork Patterns'—Ruby McKim.

'Patchwork Quilts and the Women who made them'—Ruth Finley.

'Quilts in America'—Patsy and Myron Orlofsky.

'The Romance of the Patchwork Quilt'—Carrie A. Hall and Rose G. Kretsinger.

'Sunshine and Shadow. The Amish and their Quilts'—Phyllis Haders.